Duchess of Palms

Duchess of Palms

A MEMOIR

Nadine Eckhardt

UNIVERSITY OF TEXAS PRESS · AUSTIN

First paperback edition, 2023

Requests for permission to reproduce material from this work should be sent to Permissions, University of Texas Press, Box 7819, Austin, TX 78713–7819.
utpress.utexas.edu/rp-form

♾ The paper used in this book meets the minimum requirements of ANSI/NISO Z39.48–1992 (R1997) (Permanence of Paper).

LIBRARY OF CONGRESS CATALOGING-IN-PUBLICATION DATA

Eckhardt, Nadine
Duchess of Palms : a memoir / Nadine Eckhardt. — 1st ed.
p. cm.
Includes index.
isbn 978-1-4773-2776-0 (pb : alk. paper)
1. Eckhardt, Nadine. 2. Authors' spouses—Texas—Biography.
3. Politicians' spouses—Texas—Biography. 4. Brammer, Billy Lee.
5. Eckhardt, Bob. 6. Texas—Biography. I. Title.
CT275.E2755A3 2009
976.4'063092—dc22
[B]

2008025288

DEDICATED TO ALL THE FIFTIES GIRLS

Contents

Preface

In his introduction to the 1995 University of Texas reprint of Billy Lee Brammer's *The Gay Place,* Don Graham said,

> There is a secret, as yet unwritten, history of the remarkable women of that era, bright and talented women, who came to maturity before the women's movement and who often gave up even the idea of a career for the sake of husbands who lived, as the saying goes, in a man's world.

Don Graham was right about calling the "as yet unwritten" history of *The Gay Place*–era women a "secret history." We "fifties girls" were inculcated with many conflicting messages. We thrived on movies of the forties and fifties, in which girls were sweet, virginal, sexy, demure, beautiful, perky, passive creatures that oozed perfection and would undoubtedly be perfect wives, mothers, and "helpmates." We wanted to be just like them. And we tried. Oh how we tried! And yes, we gave up even the idea of a career for the sake of husbands who lived in a man's world.

I am a fifties girl that fulfilled most of these stipulations. But if we fifties girls failed in one or two or three of these capacities, we covered up our failures through lies and manipulation, because divorce meant social and economic failure. Divorce could result in our becoming single mothers working and raising our children alone. I was also one of those wives who didn't seriously buy the prevailing social mores.

This is my story about two marriages to two semi-famous Texas men. My first husband was Bill Brammer, the novelist who wrote *The Gay Place*, a trilogy about a fictitious governor and the social political set around him, based on our experiences during the fifties working for Lyndon Baines Johnson, then the U.S. Senate majority leader. The second was Bob Eckhardt, a talented, intelligent, handsome son of a medical doctor in Austin whose forebears were from the Kleberg-Eckhardt clan and the Wurzbachs of San Antonio—well-known ranching, professional, and political families. He was a lawyer, a legislator in the Texas House of Representatives, and in 1966 he became the U.S. congressman from the 8th congressional district of Harris County and had an illustrious fifteen years in Congress.

Acknowledgments

I am grateful to my friends and family who encouraged me for years to write my memoirs. Jody Gent, Dunya Bean, and Sidney and Shelby Brammer, all wonderful editors and writers, were generous with time and suggestions. *Duchess of Palms* couldn't have gone public without the University of Texas Press people who liked the book. Tim Staley, Mary LaMotte, Allison Faust, and Katie Jones helped me along the long road to publication.

IN THE BEGINNING

IT WAS 1955. Lyndon Baines Johnson was the majority leader of the United States Senate, with his eye on the presidency. He was a conservative to some; a closet liberal to others. He knew he'd have to move to the left in order to capture the White House, which may be why he hired my twenty-seven-year-old husband, Billy Lee Brammer, then a reporter for the liberal weekly *Texas Observer,* as a pressman. I was hired as well; I had been a journalism major at the University of Texas at Austin and secretary to the editor of the *Austin American-Statesman* for a couple of years. LBJ liked to hire couples—he thought he got more out of us because, according to him, we weren't "out hoo-hawing around at night." We could work late and get to work on time. And Bill and I had liberal credentials, as we and many other young couples were pre-sixties kids ready to shed the conventions of the times.

Everyone called LBJ "The Senator." Whatever The Senator wanted, The Senator got. Horror stories circulated about the temper tantrums and tongue-lashings that occurred when something wasn't exactly to his liking. His attention to detail and power over his fellow senators gave us a lot to talk about among ourselves. Billy Lee and I were one of a number of young couples who started to work for Johnson in 1955.

Of course, as Texans, we had been aware of LBJ prior to his recent rise in power to Senate majority leader. His megapower in the U.S. Senate surprised us, because we hadn't seen him in action on the Senate floor and the control he exerted on fellow senators. LBJ was hot, and the press covered him assiduously. They even covered his staff. A feature story appeared in the August 1956 issue of the *American Weekly*, accompanied by a photo of all the couples Johnson had hired posed on the steps of the Capitol with Lady Bird and Lyndon.

When I look at the picture now, I see an exhilarated but confused young woman. How had a girl from a small town in Texas's Rio Grande Valley ended up in Washington, D.C., privy to the inner workings of the government's powerful political circles? How had circumstances propelled me, at only twenty-four, to be photographed for the *American Weekly*, standing on the steps of the Capitol, surrounded by Lyndon Johnson, the powerful U.S. Senate majority leader, and his wife? How had I ended up married to a man who would soon become one of the most well-known novelists in Texas? I could not have known then what a wild ride my life would turn out to be: that not only would I spend many years working in politics, but that later I would return to our nation's capital as the wife of a U.S. congressman. Looking back, it seems fantastic and strange—almost the stuff of fiction.

But first things first.

BIG NADINE, LITTLE NADINE: 1930S AND 1940S

The Rio Grande Valley of Texas is a large semitropical area at the southernmost tip of Texas, where the Rio Grande empties into the Gulf of Mexico. A string of towns, some with Mexican counterparts across the border, lines the river's north side for about sixty miles. The Valley lies 250 miles south of San Antonio, and it isn't hard to imagine the area having been underwater at some time—it still looks like a waterless underwater seascape. Trees, cacti, and mesquite grow low to the land in a long, gradual descent to the alluvial area, which contains some of the best farmland in the country. If watered, the rich soil blooms with too many kinds of exotic plants to count. It's hard to imagine such lushness at the other end of the long, arid drive from San Antonio.

Sometime in the late 1920s, my parents heard about the "Magic Valley" from friends. My mother, Nadine, managed a theater in Oklahoma City where my father was a theater organist. She had completed a couple of years of college; he was an organist and pianist. They did well until the talkies put my father out of work. They had a son and needed to find work, and the Great Depression was descending upon the country. A friend had a farm in the Valley, and that exotic land right next to Mexico must have sounded romantic to a couple looking for a new life. For a man used to wearing a white tux during the day and a black tux at night, the farming life would prove to be a rude shock.

I was born in a farmhouse in McAllen on January 20, 1931, and my parents divorced a year later. I have no memory of my birth father. Initially, my mother had been attracted to his musical talent and his glamorous life as a theater organist, but she soon found out about his temper, and she ended up divorcing him because of the physical abuse. I had no emotional attachment to my father, but my mother kept a large photo of him in a black tux with his hand on the organ keys, looking very suave and handsome, and I reserved a place in my heart for that image. When my mother talked about their early days together, her tone turned wistful as she remembered a time that was joyful, before the beating started. Before she had to escape.

After my mother finally left my father, she found herself stranded in the little town on the Mexican border with two children to support. The only job she could find was as a waitress at a local bar. Despite the fact that she was broke and that she later remembered this time as a low point in her life, she told stories about how wild it had been partying on both sides of the border. A series of very young Mexican maids looked after my brother Leslie and me until our mother got home. I always looked forward to her homecomings and never wanted her to leave. I needed more of her. I was two years old.

Big Nadine was in her late twenties and having a hard time in McAllen. She needed her own mother, Rose Foster. Rose was having difficulties of her own in another part of the state, where she lived on a farm in the Texas Panhandle near Pampa with her five children, Big Nadine's half brothers and sisters. The Depression definitely affected the Rio Grande Valley, but economic conditions weren't as devastating there as in other parts of the country. Big Nadine and her mother Rose decided to combine their families and hunker down in McAllen, where survival was guaranteed by fruit and vegetable crops that grew year-round and where there was potential for jobs for my two uncles and three aunts. All of us moved into a big old frame house on the edge of town. I stayed home with Grandma during the day while the grown-ups worked and pooled their money to support the family. My two uncles were bakers and worked at night. My mother and her oldest sister worked in restaurants. My mother slept late into the daytime so she could work into the evening, and I was deprived of her company. She hated the work. I liked my uncles and loved being the pet of my young aunts, Colleen and Delphine, who were only six and eight years older than I.

My brother always seemed distanced from the rest of the family. From my first memories of him, he was angry and uncooperative. He was six years older than I and was expected to do chores such as bringing the cow home after school from her grazing spot on a canal bank. He couldn't seem to follow through; he would show up at home after dark, cowless, and one of my uncles or aunts would have to finish the job. His unpleasant attitude concerned both my mother and grandmother. Mother never did figure out how to deal with him.

MY ROLE MODEL

Grandma was the fulcrum of the extended family. She cooked for all nine family members, many of whom worked at night and ate at odd times. She was probably in her early forties when I first met her as a two-year-old, and I remember telling her that her skin was too loose—she was sun-wrinkled at an early age from a life of farming. There was no Grandpa attached to Grandma; he had been a restaurant owner who had died several years earlier and was never discussed. As far as I was concerned, I sprang from Grandma and Big Nadine.

I lived with Grandma Foster from age two to age six, and during that time I absorbed some very important lessons about life. Later in my life, I realized the four years I lived with her instilled in me fundamental habits and attitudes toward life that helped me survive my mother's less-healthy influence. If anyone taught me to be happy, it was Grandma. She walked two miles every morning and fixed a good lunch afterward. She lived in the present, and I never saw her depressed. She told me about how her family had made two trips by wagon between Missouri and Texas. The children had walked and played beside the wagon as it slowly moved across the country. In her later years after all her children had married and had families of their own, Grandma had also traveled all over the United States by bus. Sometimes she took a grandchild with her on her bus rides across the country. She was healthy and lived alone for a long time; she believed that living alone solved a lot of problems, because one was forced to take care of oneself. She read constantly—anything and everything. She developed cataracts late in life and had to wait a spell before having them removed; I remember how thrilled she was when she was able to read again.

Grandma was a Republican, but when I became politically aware, I considered myself a liberal Democrat. We had many political discussions, and although we disagreed, we loved the sparring. She believed in independence and didn't file for Social Security until she was very old. To earn extra money, she babysat at a local motel.

Grandma's walking days ended when she was ninety-four. She had phlebitis and was unconscious when the decision had to be made to amputate her leg to save her life. Later she told me that she would have preferred not to live this way, but she trusted her children's decision. She never complained about her situation, even though she hated the nursing home where she lived. One day, as we sat outside, she told me that she wanted to "just keep rolling in my wheelchair, and keep going." At age ninety-nine, her organs began to shut down. Her heart kept going for four days before she finally died.

I knew that Grandma had been married to an older man, the father of my half aunts and uncles. My second husband, Bob Eckhardt, was nineteen years older than me, and one day after I had been married to him for almost fifteen years, I asked Grandma how it had been for her to be married to an older man. She replied, "It was all right for awhile. But then he started sitting around the house acting like an old man."

"What did you do?" I asked.

"I put him on the train and sent him to his sister," she answered.

Though her response sounded a bit callous, she and their children had taken the old man back when he was ill and nursed him until he died. There were no men in Grandma's life after that. When I asked her why, she said, "I just never had any use for them." No anger, no resentment . . . she just didn't need a man.

A NEW LIFE, AND NEW PROBLEMS

Along with the rest of the nation, my family began to recover during President Roosevelt's administration. As the economy started to improve, everybody drifted toward lives of their own. Auntie Ruth, who had left her new husband up in the Panhandle, went back to him. And Mother got married.

Noah was a forty-year-old bachelor, a policeman who lived with his family in a big yellow frame house on Main Street—living together to survive, much like our family. I called him Daddy Noah. He was a gentle man who took us on Sunday rides in his car, quite a treat. Mother and Noah had waited for times to get a little better before marrying, and the whole family was pleased about the union. I stayed with Grandma while they went on a brief honeymoon, and upon their return we moved into a green frame house on Broadway across the street from an ice cream factory. I was thrilled, not only about having a father but also about finally having a mother who stayed at home. I entered the first grade with a regular family; my mother made cookies for after-school snacks. I had a social life for the first time, and I made friends with other little girls. I was happy.

Daddy Noah's mother, a large woman who was a constant fixture on the front porch of the yellow frame house on Main Street, seemed very old to me at the time. My mother considered her in-laws "country" and was never close to them. She had her own mother and half brothers and sisters, and we all visited frequently. My parents ate out at Sam's Place, their favorite restaurant in Reynosa, the Mexican counterpart to McAllen. They took me along and I would sing "Pennies From Heaven" for the proprietor or their friends. Big Nadine made sure I took violin and tap-dancing lessons, though I don't know who enjoyed them more, she or I.

My brother Leslie was a problem for Big Nadine and Daddy Noah. His grades were low and he didn't attract friends. We fought a lot, more than most siblings. When he started attempting to molest me sexually, I began to truly hate him. I escaped his advances only because he was physically small and not very smart, and I wasn't an easy mark. I have often wondered what would've happened if I had actually felt affection for him or had any respect for him as an older brother. My mother told me he was also a victim of our father's temper and abuse. He was obviously damaged early on, somehow, and never successfully coped with his life.

The mystery to me is why I didn't tell my mother and stepfather about Leslie's advances. It wasn't until I was in my forties that I told my mother, and when she asked why I hadn't done so earlier, I found myself at a loss to explain. The shame and guilt and anger that I had felt at the time had been so frightening. Although I hadn't "done anything," I still kept everything deep inside. From what I've read about incest, this is a common reaction in kids who have been victims or near-victims. Nevertheless, the situation was a blight on my childhood that created a deep distrust, scorn, and anger toward my brother that persisted for many years.

I now believe that Leslie's attempts at molestation were borne of a desire to harm me. He was jealous of my friends, my grades, and my mother's obvious delight in the fact that I was a happy little kid. I shudder to think what could've happened if I hadn't already developed some self-confidence through an active social life, a nurturing mother and father, and a happy school life. But the situation still harmed me—the mere intent harms. These days incest is less taboo to discuss; now that women have become allies instead of adversaries, we share our life experiences. It is startling to find out how many women have been sexual targets within their own families. I know how it affected me; I can't imagine what damage would've resulted from a truly incestuous relationship.

BIG NADINE

My mother was beautiful and smart, with a certain classy style—she was always well dressed and groomed—but even with assets like these she was still unhappy at times. She adhered to the female ideal of the 1920s and 30s: she wanted to marry a good provider and never have to worry about working for a living again. When she married Daddy Noah, she seemed content to be the complete housewife. She prepared wonderful meals in her red, black, and white 1940s kitchen with its gleaming Chambers range. Homemade Parker House rolls, pork roasts, and candied yams came out of the kitchen on Sundays. On Monday, wash day, she washed the clothes in her washing machine in the garage, rolling them through the wringer and then hanging them on the clothesline. The linens went through the funny-looking ironing machine that pressed them between two heated rollers, resulting in perfectly smooth sheets and pillowcases. The lace tablecloth came off the dining table three times a day, replaced by one made in Mexico with matching napkins made of rough, durable material embroidered with Mexican Aztec designs. During the hot summers, sometimes we would have only ice cream for dinner, hand-cranked in the ice cream machine and covered with homemade chocolate sauce and pecans.

Big Nadine was the only child born during Grandma's first marriage to Bert Thompson, a professional gambler, whose mother was a full-blooded Cherokee. She was better educated, and her expectations were different. Sometimes she yearned for a more exciting life, but in spite of this longing she was grateful for Noah, the good man she had married, who had a consistent personality and no temper.

What I adopted and integrated into my personality from my Grandma couldn't be erased. She was practical in every way. She cared not for "décor." She was outspoken and unconcerned about what others thought, whereas my mother was too concerned about appearance and what other people thought. But my independence began to be overlaid with Big Nadine's expectations and aspirations for life as we moved into our respective new positions as the wife and adopted children of Noah Cannon. My mother was generally happy, and she was prettier than other mothers and better dressed. She wore cute linen dresses and colorful Mexican sandals in the summer and kept herself well groomed. There was something about her that harkened back to an earlier, more glamorous time. She talked about the Orpheum Circuit, a booking agency of that era, and how she had met Pola Negri, the silent movie star, at the theater in Oklahoma City. Although she didn't have money, she applied her talents to make her life in McAllen as comfortable and pleasant as possible.

My mother's years as a waitress weighed on her; she seemed to feel stigmatized by having done (as she viewed it) such "lowly" work. She married Daddy Noah with the expectation of never having to work again, but when World War II arrived and took many men from McAllen, my mother replaced the male manager of the Queen Theater. Although she professed that she didn't want to work, she obviously enjoyed being out in the public and spending time with the young people who worked at the theater. Managing the Queen during the war years brought positive feelings connected to independence and self-worth back to Big Nadine, but she felt uncomfortable about having strayed from the genteel picture she had in her mind of the ideal woman of her era. She also seemed to feel conflicted about not being at home to cater to Daddy Noah, my brother, and me. I knew her spirits were higher during the times she worked outside our home, but I grew up with the impression that such work was a sign of feminine failure. Success, I concluded, meant finding the right provider. There were three fundamental messages regarding work that I got from my mother: 1) working for a living was not okay, which meant that independence was not okay either; 2) working could be fun and spiritually and emotionally uplifting; and 3) letting your work take you away from your family is bad and should make you feel neglectful. I couldn't pack any more contradictions into those three short lessons if I tried.

As much self-confidence as work brought her, my mother did not translate that feeling into self-esteem. I don't think she ever considered working again. Like many other women after World War II, she vanished back into her home, where she felt more comfortable, less threatened, and, on the surface, genteel. Most important, she no longer felt guilt.

My world enlarged dramatically after I started the first grade. Everything seemed perfect. I loved my Daddy Noah, who came and went on schedule—he came home for lunch, took a little siesta, and went back to work, dropping me off at school on his way. He had been in the Valley since he left his family farm in Kenedy, Texas, in the 1920s. He was a steady, good-looking, kind man who had learned Spanish from his Mexican fellow policemen, and he never got upset over little things. I knew he loved me, and I loved him, but I always reserved a little compartment of love for my "real" father. This must have kept me at some distance from Daddy Noah, but he never appeared to notice it, and he treated me as his daughter in every way.

Daddy Noah soon became the chief of police of McAllen, and he stayed Chief Cannon throughout most of my high-school years.

This fit right in with my mother's concepts of social acceptability. She was proud of him and proud to be his wife. His position meant a great deal to her, and she wanted my brother and me to live up to standards befitting the children of the chief of police. They built a new house in the late 1930s—white with green shutters and hardwood floors. Newly furnished throughout, the house was their pride and joy. Mother bragged about how her bedroom suite was custom-designed and how the dining room suite was "red-rock maple." Not just any old furniture would do—it had to be special. But in spite of the material comfort a new house and furniture may have provided, I eventually came to the realization that, for my mother, McAllen just didn't cut it. She still yearned for something more.

GROWING UP, IN BODY AND MIND

In September of 1939, my fifth-grade teacher announced that it was a sad day—Poland had fallen to the Nazis. War bonds were sold in the schools, and we were told that our country was being threatened. When the United States entered the war and mobilization got underway, my brother enlisted in the Navy. This solved the Leslie problem for the immediate future. He actually did do some growing up in the Navy, but after the war his problems persisted.

At that point, happiness to me was playing with my cats and my friends and making good grades. We rode bicycles, had sleepovers, and played softball. Kids ran in a neighborhood pack. We played hide-and-go-seek in the summer until the grown-ups called us in to go to bed. We ran up and down the alleys and called each other out to play. Everybody knew everybody—whom to pick and not to pick for your team, who was a crybaby, who tattled.

One day I overheard my aunts talking about me.

"I wonder what she'll be when she grows up," one said.

"I don't know, but she'll be something," said the other. This made me feel incredibly special and accepted. The aunts were in their teens at the time, dating young airmen from Moore Field Air Force Base and working at the other movie theater in McAllen, the Palace. Movies played a major role in our lives. Since my mother worked at the Queen, I often watched movies while waiting for her—I had my first sexual feelings watching Gene Autry sing by the campfire. Because my mother also loved movies, we usually attended at least one a week. My girlfriends and I discussed weekly which movie star we had a crush on, emulating movie stars' looks and actions. Many years later, I noticed that one of my old classmates had a walk much like Robert Mitchum's, and I teased him that he had seen too many Robert Mitchum movies. He admitted that he had adopted that walk as a teenager and had been walking around like that ever since! (Movies and music are even more powerful in our lives today. The moment I saw Bill Clinton curl his lip, I knew he had seen a lot of Elvis films. It won him both the female vote and the ire of the Republicans.)

During those war years, Leslie brought Navy sailors home with him, and my parents would host barbecues in the backyard. Everyone was excited about the war—McAllen would have been awfully dull without it. Big Nadine enjoyed preparing for these weekends, and Daddy Noah made sure that we had birds and venison to barbecue. Everyone did what they thought was their patriotic duty to support the war effort.

By the time I was thirteen, I was boy-crazy, running around with my girlfriends, flirting with the cutest, nicest boys, and feeling insecure about whether or not they liked me. There were social clubs and a recreation hall called the Fox Hole, where the kids could gather and dance to a jukebox. We danced to "One O'Clock Jump," and Dickey Harris gave me my first kiss, planting it on my forehead as we danced at the Fox Hole.

The happiest time in my life was just before I hit puberty, when I had no conscious gender identification and was simply a happy animal with little self-consciousness. Life was uncomplicated and serene. When boys started giving me valentines, Christmas gifts, etc., I wondered why they were paying so much attention. I felt unaffected by it until, after noticing the envy of my girlfriends,

I realized that my effect on boys was a form of power. Even so, I took on the prevailing cultural practice of showering attention on males. I learned to juggle the endless stream of men and somehow, in my confused way, I felt I had to be absolutely wonderful for each and all. Many females of that era did the same thing. We fifties girls matured during the rise of Frank Sinatra's popularity, and we believed what we heard in songs—never mind what our parents told us about good character and conduct. We heard Frank Sinatra beckon us to his libertine lifestyle, yet we were supposed to be "perfect" for our men. We listened to Sinatra sing, "The girl that I marry will have to be as soft and pink as a nursery, the girl I call my own will wear satin and laces and smell of cologne," and we complied with his request. I wore a pink angora sweater, smelled of cologne, and dreamed of my very own Sinatra to romp and play with. Between Sinatra and Scarlett O'Hara, the war and economic challenges, young women of the fifties were a very confused generation—we had so many conflicting messages aimed at us, yet we managed to survive.

Sex—penetration, anyway—was simply not acceptable. It was avoided or postponed by going out in groups of four or six. Going out meant dressing up and being picked up by your date at home, and introducing him to your folks before driving the seven miles to the international bridge at Reynosa. In Reynosa, we had a choice of nightclubs with bands, floor shows, and anything we wanted to drink no matter what age we were. The Monte Carlo was a restaurant with a giant patio dance floor with a huge band shell at one end and a long bar at the other. It touted itself as having the largest patio in the world and it probably did. Good dancers from the little towns up and down the Valley gravitated to the same places we did to dance the jitterbug, rumba, and samba in our high heels, dancing backward doing the tango, returning to our table to sip Zombies, Hurricanes, or some other lethal concoction.

I was a late bloomer in the physical sense; while the other girls' breasts blossomed forth, my chest remained flat. We all had names to describe our breasts—or lack thereof—and I was known as "tortilla flat." (I remedied this in 1960 when I bought breast implants—before silicone, thank God. Now they are antique and more or less invisible.) I managed to avoid real sex no matter how much tequila I drank, until curiosity and competitiveness with my girlfriends got the best of me. I had my first sexual intercourse with a boy to whom I was sexually attracted, but it was messy and painful, not what I had expected. I didn't want to go out with him again. I was too young to date Air Force flyboys during the war, and for this my mother was grateful.

By the time I was through with high school in 1948, I had been nominated Freshman Queen, dated untold numbers of boys, had sex, and been chosen Duchess of Palms by audience applause at the Palace Theater—the ultimate honor for a seventeen-year-old McAllen girl. This meant I was to represent McAllen in the annual Citrus Fiesta, a Valley-wide celebration of the citrus industry. My picture was in the newspapers, and the Chamber of Commerce gave me one hundred dollars for a gown of my choice, which was palm green, of course. A strapless metallic blue bathing suit totally unsuited for water was my favorite prize. My mother enjoyed every minute of all this, and I loved being Miss Hot Shit, but later on I omitted that part of my past in conversation because I feared being ridiculed by my college friends.

Around this time I realized that there wasn't much more to do in the Magic Valley other than get married. I was ready to get away. My friends were going to school in places like Virginia and Missouri, and it was a rude shock to find out that my parents didn't have the means for me to go to college. Daddy Noah enrolled me in business college, but I only lasted three days. I was depressed about this, so I tried another tack, enrolling in a junior college ten miles away and hitching rides with friends. I took art, algebra, shorthand, and business law. During the summer of 1949 I got a job in a drugstore and saved my money, which enabled me to enroll at North Texas State College in Denton, Texas, now known as the University of North Texas.

At North Texas I was an art major. I loved the campus and my classes, but what I really loved was the freedom of being away from my mother. I cut my hair off à la Ingrid Bergman in *For Whom the Bell Tolls*; I wore earrings and Mexican shoes. I was rushed by several sororities and spent every free moment with guys, at coffee date after coffee date. I don't recall ever cleaning my room. I was a pig, in rebellion against my compulsive mother, who had kept everything so neat and clean.

My friend Bruce Henderson, who was like a brother to me, was editor of the *Campus Chat*, the school paper. For the Christmas edition, he sent a photographer over to shoot me under the dorm Christmas tree in my blue metallic bathing suit, smiling up at a cute fraternity boy who feigned surprise at finding such a "present." Bruce also introduced me to someone he very much admired because, as Bruce said, "Bill is an intellectual *and* an athlete." As it turned out, Bruce was right. I had never met anyone like Billy Lee Brammer.

BILLY LEE BRAMMER, 1950

Bill was christened "Billy Lee" by Kate and H.L. (Herbert Leslie) Brammer, as if they knew he would be their pet, their sweet little troublemaker, their last child. Kate was almost past menopause when Billy Lee was born, and as a little boy he felt guilty when his mother would break into tears over his small infractions. He was much loved and indulged by Kate and H.L., even though he came along on April 21, 1929, at about the same time that the Depression arrived full swing in Oak Cliff, then a suburb of Dallas.

H.L. was a mid-level executive with the Dallas Power and Light Company, and the family lived at 922 South Windomere Street, one of a row of identical houses. Billy Lee lived up to his name. He was a bright, sweet, lovable little boy, perceived as unique and talented by all. He had plenty of playmates on South Windomere Street. Kate stayed home with him during his early years, and he was in many ways an only child, as his brother and sister were older and had already left home. Later on, however, during World War II, Kate went to work, as many housewives did, which left Billy

Lee with much unsupervised time on his hands. He was a natural athlete with a strong physique, on the short side (about five feet seven inches tall), with big brown eyes and wavy brown hair. He wasn't conventionally handsome, but his whole effect was very sensual and attractive to women. While I was growing up in the Rio Grande Valley, dating, dancing, and drinking in Mexico, Billy Lee was teaching himself how to type by copying short stories by Ernest Hemingway.

When Bill and I first started dating, he was just getting over losing a girlfriend who had dumped him for Skippy Browning, an Olympic diver from Dallas. The rejection motivated him to become an accomplished swimmer and diver in order to get the girl back. It didn't work. This story resonated with me years later when I was already separated and emotionally removed from him, and he performed a marathon writing binge that produced *The Gay Place*.

We both rebelled against the status quo, but in different ways. Billy stayed out of high school for a whole semester without his parents knowing. While Kate was gone in the afternoons, boys and girls congregated over at Billy's house to do what boys and girls do. We were both very conscious of the racism that surrounded us in our respective hometowns. The Valley essentially had—and still has—a class system based on cheap Mexican labor. In Dallas, blacks comprised a large part of the population. Billy told me how ashamed he felt after throwing rotten tomatoes at them on the street as he rode around with his less-sensitive buddies in Oak Cliff.

Billy enrolled at the University of Texas in 1947 as a journalism major, and later transferred to North Texas State College. He felt small and insignificant next to the more mature veterans who had returned to continue their interrupted educations; he complained that it was hard to date girls because they preferred the older guys. He was a voracious reader for his entire life. As a journalism major and an athlete, sports writing came to him naturally, and he began to write professionally about sports for the *Denton Record-Chronicle*.

When I first met Billy Lee in early 1950 in the NTSC *Campus Chat* offices (Bruce Henderson had arranged for a meeting), I was not impressed. Until he spoke. He was incredibly well-read and extremely witty. His sense of humor displayed a profound intellectual depth unusual in men of that age—especially the men I had known in the Valley. He was insatiably curious about the world and had an adventurous spirit. Bill, as he was then called (at that time I was unaware of his birth name), looked to me like a Dallas hood, or a pachuco from the Valley. He had a ducktail haircut, blue suede shoes, and a slouchy walk. He wore his collar turned up.

Bruce, Bill, and I hung out often, talking about politics and making fun of sororities and fraternities, even though Bill and I had both pledged. (We were uncooperative pledges, but we did, in the end, become members. We weren't in total rebellion against the status quo.) Bill lived off campus, with two apartment-mates. Each week too many of us would cram into the bedroom to watch Milton Berle on a little black-and-white set.

The U.S. government's response to Communist government in Russia after World War II was fear. In 1950, college students had to sign a loyalty oath when enrolling for classes swearing loyalty only to the United States. It was unnecessary because Communism was just an idea to which our government was overreacting, we thought. World War II had ended only five years before the Korean War started under President Truman's administration. Bill missed the draft by getting married on April 20, 1950, the day before his twenty-first birthday.

To young people having fun and learning about new ideas in economics and sociology, the Korean War seemed to be a vague and far off issue. But the world had shrunk and avant-garde art and social experiment from Europe were emanating to U.S. campuses, attracting young people like us who were bored with our provincialism and wanted to broaden our horizons. We yearned to go to Europe, sit in sidewalk cafés, paint, write, and discuss issues with other expatriates. Instead, we drank Pernod (since we couldn't go to Paris), listened to "Bólero," smoked cigarettes, and ate Mexican food.

Bill and I discussed living together and/or bumming around

Europe, but our middle-class backgrounds prevailed. We were just bizarre enough for each other. I could never have married a Valley boy, and Bill was attracted to the restlessness that simmered just under my seemingly sweet persona: the *picante*. He even encouraged it. One night he told me that I needed to speak all the words I was avoiding. He said, "I want you to yell 'shit' as loud as you can yell it, so you can understand what I'm telling you." We drove around the square in Denton, with me hollering "shit!" as loud as I could.

The North Texas campus may have been beautiful, but my grades didn't look too good. Rather than spending time in the art lab, I was dancing with Bill to the music of the renowned North Texas Lab Band, who played Thursday afternoons at the student union. Bill had rhythm, and we both loved to dance. I was spending too much time with Bill and Bruce, drinking Cointreau and Tom Collins mix—God forbid! We didn't have access to mind-altering drugs at the time, but if we had, we'd have been taking them.

I had strong feelings for Bill; he stimulated my mind. But I had a whole other life in the Valley, where I could marry some eligible young man and have a comfortable life. During Easter vacation of 1950, at home in McAllen, I took a measured look at the men there. (I felt detached.)

After the holidays, I was returning to school with some friends in an open Oldsmobile convertible, cruising the 250-mile stretch of highway between the Valley and San Antonio. We were driving too fast, passing cars on the wrong side of the road, beer cans flying out of the car, when someone said, "Hey, was that Bill Brammer in that Chevy that just went by?"

I made my friends turn around. I was shocked that Bill would drive six hundred miles just to see me. He stopped and backed up to talk.

"What the hell are you doing here?" I asked.

"Driving you back to school," he replied.

In retrospect, it was a meaningful moment. I said good-bye to the Rio Grande Valley when I got in Bill's car, waved to my friends, and sped away to the strains of "Rag Mop."

By the time we got to Denton, we had discussed the advantages and disadvantages of living together and had realized that it just wouldn't work in 1950s Texas. We decided we could get married and continue school if we were both working. Even though I consented to marry Bill, I was conflicted. Part of me wanted to be with him, but part of me wanted to be free. I was enjoying my life, but I was at a point where I needed some direction, whether I knew it or not. Call it impulse, intuition, insanity—whatever it was, our decision to marry was not rational. Did we think about each other's personalities or personal goals? Did we reach any kind of mutual agreement about what we wanted? No. What we wanted was to continue being dependents, but at the same time to have our freedom. My parents were unable to finance my college education, so I knew I would have to work. I figured Bill and I could manage if we both worked part-time and went to school part-time. Besides having this basic survival plan figured out, I had only a vague idea of what I was doing. Bill seemed to be more certain than I was that this union was meant to be.

YOUNG MARRIEDS

We got married on April 20, 1950—the day before Bill's twenty-first birthday. I was nineteen. We eloped to Lewisville, Texas, where we interrupted the one-legged judge's game of dominoes. We were pronounced husband and wife while a little boy yelled his testimonial in a tent revival meeting across the street. The scene was bizarre and a bit depressing. We spent the night in a motel and were back at school on Monday.

My mother lost five pounds the week I told her I had gotten married, but the Brammers took it fairly well. We rented a tiny apartment near campus and continued attending school. All we did was study and have sex; we both made the dean's list for the first time. We lived on tacos and Coke, since that's all I knew how to fix. (Bill's diet also included candy bars and Benzedrine.) We visited Kate and H.L.'s house in Dallas frequently; they were nurturing and supportive. Bill was still their baby. Mr. Brammer could never say no to Bill, and insisted on giving him money when we were there. Once, he gave Bill a mint-condition Chevrolet, which Bill traded for a used Pontiac a few months later.

We had gotten our way—we were still dependents, to a degree, but we were also able to be together. I got a job as secretary to the director of the journalism department at North Texas and switched my major to journalism. I helped Bill pass Spanish, and he helped me get through journalism. In 1951, we moved to Corpus Christi so Bill could intern for the *Corpus Christi Caller-Times*. Bill took a correspondence course on the Bible (a snap course if there ever was one) in order to gain the credits he needed to graduate; he received his diploma by mail from North Texas State College. Bill worked in the *Caller-Times* sports department, and I worked as a secretary for an independent oilman. We didn't know anyone in Corpus, so we hung out together, went to Padre Island, and read books.

It wasn't long before we tired of the real world and decided to get back on the school track. In the summer of 1951, we both enrolled at the University of Texas at Austin. Bill got a job in the sports department at the *Austin American-Statesman,* and I worked for the director of the School of Architecture at UT. I was happy going to school and working.

Three months into the semester, I began to feel sick and lethargic. Opening the cat food brought on nausea. At first I thought we had a gas leak, but the doctor said, "There's nothing wrong with a healthy girl like you. You're pregnant." My mother suggested I come home so she could take care of me until I got over my pregnancy nausea. I hated taking the time away from school and my job, but I stayed with my parents for several weeks until my nausea was over. I returned to Austin to a cute little rental Bill had set up, with enough room for a baby.

Bill was constantly restless. He was also constantly broke. But since he was the man, and it was the 1950s, I assumed that he would take on the family's financial responsibility and that I didn't worry about that aspect of our lives. Later in our marriage, I realized that

Bill was entirely unable to manage money. He spent foolishly—compulsively. He bought things on credit; life became a constant search for money to pay off what he had already bought. He bought nine cars in six years, everything from a Morris Minor to a Jaguar to a Plymouth station wagon. Not until I had children, and gradually realized that I had to take responsibility, did I confront him about his spending habits. I wanted to stay home with our children and not work, and I could see that this would be impossible as long as Bill was racking up bills.

But he continued to shop. He knew every new product that came on the market; we had a Waring blender before anyone else on the block. I knew we were doing something wrong—we could barely pay for necessities like food and gasoline—but it didn't occur to me to assert myself and tell Bill to control his spending. Fifties women played passive roles. We looked to men for guidance and expected them to take care of us, and we often felt helpless.

My pregnancy meant that I wouldn't be able to go back to school, and this was very upsetting to me. My mother suggested that I get an abortion so I could resume my education. In fact, at one point I tried to take some medicine that would make me abort; Bill called me when I was about to take it. When I told him what I was doing, he talked me out of it by promising that I could continue my education after the baby's birth. He always wanted children; I didn't. My mother empathized with me—she knew I wasn't ready for motherhood. She also knew that Bill was irresponsible and that I needed to prepare myself for the future by completing a college education. But she didn't interfere with our decision. I had faith—Bill would become a famous novelist, while I would be the enigmatic wife. Any idea of going back to college eventually became dormant, at least for the next decade. My vague hopes for Bill's success as an author displaced my own ambition to get a degree, and I resigned myself to simply being a good "helpmate," as we were called in the fifties, to my husband.

On August 11, 1952, our beautiful baby girl was born. We named her Sidney Gail. By the time Sidney was nine months old, I had to go back to work. We needed the money. This was my initiation as a working mother, and I hated it. I enjoyed the job working for the editor of the *Austin American-Statesman*, but I felt sad and negligent because I was away from Sidney all day.

TESTING THE WATERS, PUSHING THE BOUNDARIES

During this time I discovered F. Scott Fitzgerald and read every book by or about him. I identified with his wife Zelda, an engaging southern girl with artistic aspirations of her own. Zelda, along with Hemingway's Lady Brett Ashley and Michael Arlen's Iris March of *The Green Hat*, were elusive, quixotic, and irresistible to men. They were romanticized in such beautifully written books . . . I wanted to be like them, even though they were confused, depressed, and ambivalent about their relationships. The authors, who were close to the real-life counterparts of these characters, wrote about them in an attempt to support and understand them. I too was married to an aspiring writer who wanted to understand me, but like the enigmatic women of those stories, I didn't understand myself.

While our personal and financial problems simmered underneath the surface, Bill's professional life prospered. He moved from writing sports to the editorial side of the paper and won statewide awards for writing features. Everyone loved Bill; he was charming, witty, gentle, and nonthreatening, indulged by parents, friends, and coworkers. Men liked him because he could talk sports and was athletic, intelligent, and naughty. Women liked him because he asked questions about their lives and actually listened when they answered—and because he was naughty. (Later on, I found his intense questioning intrusive and sometimes felt that it verged on voyeurism. Sometimes Bill would set me up in conversations so he could watch me interact with various attractive male friends. If I met someone at a party and engaged them in conversation, he would quiz me on it when we got home. In current psychological terms, he didn't respect my boundaries. I would never have allowed this if I had been aware at the time of my right to protect my boundaries.

Years later, Bill's second wife, Dorothy, told me that he had done the same thing with her.)

Things were going well for Bill, but even though he was advancing professionally, his salary was still fairly low. Newspaper people never make much money. But my salary helped us gain a feeling of being middle-class, and we had a house and child, so our parents began to accept us as adults. On August 31, 1954, two years after I had Sidney, I gave birth to another baby girl, Shelby. Responsibilities at home increased. Our income was reduced by one salary, since the economics of my returning to work did not play out: if I paid someone to take care of the girls, all the income from my salary would go toward employing that person, with no money left over. The only alternative was that Bill had to find a job that paid more so I could stay home with the girls. Then Bill found a house for $8,500 on a little street near Deep Eddy Pool off Lake Austin Boulevard, where I took Sidney and Shelby swimming most summer days. Around this time I had a Nash Rambler convertible that I loved; it was the first automobile that I ever considered mine. One day Bill came home with a new Plymouth station wagon. When I asked how he got it, he said, "Oh, I traded in the convertible for it." I was furious. He rationalized the purchase by saying we needed it to haul Sidney's playpen. I was learning the hard way about it being a "man's world."

But this was an interesting period in our lives. We were having a great time socially in Austin, but a horrible time financially. We were part of a set of young, sexually progressive married couples who were the Texas version of Jack Kerouac's Beat Generation. We were in love with romance, decadence, politics, and literature. We read competitively with various members of one set to be witty and sparkling in the most esoteric way. The set included law students, artists, legislators, and youngish professors at UT. Austin was small enough for us to know about each other. Everyone had small children and responsibilities, but we managed to cluster at watering holes like Scholz Garten in Austin, at each other's homes, and at house parties on ranches. We wives took the children to swim every day in spring-fed swimming holes and sat on quilts, gossiping and nurturing our tans. We were humanists—we had faith in human beings, not God or "the spirit." We believed in education and knowledge and reveled in health and beauty.

The men in the group didn't want to be The Man in the Gray Flannel Suit—they wanted to fulfill some kind of vague myth, whether it be the myth of the hard-drinking, hard-drugging, womanizing writer, like Kerouac, or the myth of the hard-drinking, hard-drugging, womanizing cowboy-landed-gentry, like a John Wayne character (but with a degree in philosophy). They wanted to become whatever fantasies they possessed. Some of these men peaked early, like Willie Morris, who became the youngest editor of *Harper's Magazine* at thirty-two; Bill, whose book *The Gay Place* was published when he was twenty-nine; and Ronnie Dugger, who was editor of the *Texas Observer* at twenty-four. (All three had worked for the *Observer* at some point.) The women in the group simply aspired to perfection—or at least the *appearance* of perfection.

Our sexual relationships were changing along with the times, and we began to experiment in other, more potentially destructive ways—not just to talk the talk, but to walk the walk. We lied to ourselves and to each other, swapped partners, and acted on our own selfish motivations, doing whatever we wanted to when we wanted to, and rationalizing it later with intellectual verbiage. We discussed everything, and whether it was politics or sleeping with someone else's wife or husband, we couched it in clever repartee and witty put-downs, served with plenty of alcohol. If we slept with someone else's husband, we were discreet; we maintained the facade. We were hypocritical and manipulative. At our weekend parties on ranches, we drank martinis and gin-and-tonics before dinner and brandy afterward, argued about politics and art, felt up each other's wives and husbands, and then headed back to town for the week.

Bill and I enjoyed this lifestyle of fun and games for a while, but eventually he became uncomfortable with it. He saw me enjoying myself, taking care of the girls, swimming every day, and partying on the weekends, and he felt the pressure to bring in more money to stay on par with some of our friends, who were either from wealthy families or were making more money in their jobs.

In 1954, a liberal Texas weekly called the *Texas Observer* was founded by Frankie Randolph, a wealthy woman from Houston. The *Observer*'s editor, Ronnie Dugger, offered Bill a job; Bill was intrigued and immediately quit the *Austin American-Statesman*. Thus began our long friendship with Ronnie and Jean Dugger, who later became Mrs. Robert Sherrill. After working for a corporate newspaper monopoly, Bill enjoyed the freedom of writing for a liberal weekly, and he and Ronnie did some excellent work together. They covered politics and the Texas legislature with a different mission: to report on the cronyism and sleazy politics that profited the politicians and their patrons. Consequently, the *Observer* gained the respect of politicians and lobbyists, which remains true to this day.

Later, when I was working in Washington, LBJ requested to see the *Observer* when it arrived. After he had his heart attack, I joked that I had reservations about handing it over—the *Observer* didn't cut Lyndon any slack. The *Observer* still labors along in its uphill battle, tackling important news that the dailies ignore.

Our financial dilemmas didn't improve with the *Observer* job, however, and Bill began to actively search for another one. After hearing that LBJ was looking to hire a Texas pressman, Bill talked to someone in his office, and was hired. Soon thereafter, I had an interview with Walter Jenkins, Johnson's right-hand man, and was hired as well. Some of our friends gave us a hard time about these new jobs; in our Austin circles LBJ was considered very conservative, which says a lot about the attitude of young Austin liberals in the fifties. But we were excited about our new prospects, and in January of 1955 we packed up, rented our little house to a couple, and the girls and I winged away on a cushy, luxe Brown & Root plane to join Bill, who had preceded us, in Washington, D.C.

1955–1961: A WILD RIDE IN WASHINGTON

Bill and I might've been more intimidated by D.C. and its trappings if we had been less-sophisticated young people. We were twenty-four and twenty-six. Growing up on small-town politics in bicultural South Texas, experiencing 1950s Austin, and living my life on intuition served me well with LBJ. I knew I didn't want to be obligated to this older man (he seemed old to me even though he was only forty-seven) who seemed to strike fear in everyone's hearts. If he came through the office and he saw a cluttered desk, the former schoolteacher in him verbally rapped the knuckles of the whole office while making the offender into an object lesson. Why he blew up like that was unknown. I never felt uneasy around him, and I enjoyed him when he talked softly and instructively to me without any sexual innuendo.

Senator Johnson's staff was terrific, a well-functioning public relations operation; it was considered the best on the Hill. LBJ was his own best staff person—a picky Virgo—with excellent insights and a hands-on (some said *too* hands-on) management style. He was involved in every aspect of his operation. For example, he had a rule that all mail must be answered before anyone went home at night. We would compose the replies, Johnson would read everything, noting corrections in the margins in a beautiful, legible handwriting, reminding us that he'd been a schoolteacher before becoming an elected politician. The whole operation was geared to make him seem ubiquitous, placing the emphasis on the personal in political dealings, even with those he knew casually.

Staff who wrote letters for him had to be acquainted with both his distinctive writing style and his relationship with whoever had written to him. Billy Lee was in the odd position of having to pen a daily chatty note from LBJ to his mother, Rebekah Baines Johnson. The whole operation was a sleight of hand, a manipulation to make people think Johnson was their sincere friend. Of course, all politicians do this to a degree, or at least try. We wrote parodies of these letters to our friends, ending them with Johnson's usual, "You are my friend, my friend," and various other corny LBJ-isms. (Years later, as a congressional wife, I confess that I used some of these same deceptive techniques when Bob wouldn't answer his mail.) LBJ's all-encompassing control over his domain extended even to the point of giving his secretary/mistress, who wasn't as svelte as he desired, fifty dollars for every pound she lost.

MEETING "THE SENATOR"

Grace Tully, who had been one of Franklin Roosevelt's secretaries, worked in the same suite I did and she took me under her wing. A beautiful Irishwoman, Grace wore stylish 1940s dresses made of fine fabrics and decorated with sequined flowers. She wrote letters for LBJ and knew everyone of any consequence in Washington, D.C., from the New Deal days. One day she interrupted me at my desk to say, "I want you to meet Mrs. Roosevelt, Nadine." And there she was, Eleanor Roosevelt, shaking my hand and asking me what I was working on. She was smaller than I would've guessed, wearing a pastel, flowered, little-old-lady dress. Her fingernails were painted crimson, an interesting juxtaposition with the grandmotherly outfit. She was warm and friendly, and I felt very much at ease. Soon after they left, the phone rang and The Senator (I hadn't met him personally at that point) said, "Honey [he called all women 'Honey'], do you want to come down to mah office for a little birthday party for Mrs. Roosevelt?"

The scene in LBJ's majority leader's office off the Senate Gallery was memorable. The room, with its gorgeous chandelier, gilded mirror, and fireplace, was carpeted and decorated in the moss greens decorators favored in the fifties. Mrs. Roosevelt, Grace, and a few other staff members were chatting, and at the center of the room stood The Senator. Senators Stuart Symington, Hubert Humphrey, and Theodore Green were milling around a fire that crackled in the fireplace and sidling up to a bar that had been set up across the room from Lyndon's huge desk. Everyone grew mellow on Scotch (LBJ's staffers knew just how to mix his Scotch and water), and Lyndon made his way around to introduce himself. He had large, soft-brown eyes that were magnified by his bifocals. Jiggling the change in his pocket constantly, he asked me questions: "What does your daddy do?" and "How do you like your job?" His attention was flattering, his charm and charisma considerable.

I desperately wanted to talk to Senator Humphrey; he was my political hero at the time. Senator Humphrey and I were engaged in conversation when suddenly The Senator hollered rudely across the room, "Hubert!" He snapped his fingers like he was calling a dog. Senator Humphrey bolted across the room to Lyndon's side as if he had a spring in his ass, and my respect for him diminished a bit. Years later, when Johnson discounted Humphrey's virtues as vice president, I remembered not only Lyndon's behavior at Mrs. Roosevelt's birthday party, but also Hubert's seeming willingness to let him do it.

WANDERING EYES AND HANDS

Johnson and two of his secretaries occupied the ornate majority leader's office in the Capitol. More staff was headquartered in the Senate Office Building in the Democratic Policy Committee Room and the Texas office, a series of rooms occupied by secretaries transcribing endless letters. Plus, there was Johnson's private, meticulously decorated hideaway in the Capitol basement. Everyone, including the Capitol guards, knew that this hideaway was where Johnson had his trysts with willing women.

Johnson's lechery was frequently a topic of conversation among the staff. We didn't have a word for it then, but we do now: sexual harassment. Sexual harassment was so common and accepted in the 1950s that we hardly acknowledged it, except to joke about it occasionally. LBJ could grope your whole body in a split second; this once happened to me as he "helped" me get out of the backseat of a car. It's so strange how we women put up with this kind of behavior in the fifties. When LBJ asked, "When're you and me gonna have a drink?" I was tactful and hid behind my marriage, saying, "Why, Bill and I would love to have a drink with you, anytime." Over the years, I have discussed LBJ's behavior with other women. In spite of the man's lecherous ways, I liked him; this is a common refrain among women who knew him. We all liked him personally and approved of much of what he accomplished, in spite of the part of him that was outrageous, crude, and unwelcome. Perhaps he suffered some kind of confusion—did he think he was flattering the women he hit on? Or did he think that if he tried all of them, sooner or later he'd score?

I had never stopped feeling ambivalent about my marriage, and I yearned to be single, but the thought of life as a single parent with two little girls was terrifying. I felt love for Bill, but I was regretful that I hadn't gotten a degree, and resentful that I was expected to carry the entire domestic load. Money was a constant source of worry. (A letter to me from Bill from this period begins, "Here is some business for which we have no funds. Note we bounced our first check at National Capital. Hope the two checks I wrote in Austin clear through here . . .") And, more importantly, I was already straying sexually and emotionally, and had had several flings by the time the photo on the steps of the Capitol was taken in 1956. In it I look dazed and confused. I was.

It wasn't long before I was experiencing the high that comes from flirting with new, exciting men. I had been assigned to the office of George Reedy, LBJ's national pressman, in the Capitol. My job was to compile all of LBJ's past speeches. Older staffers, mostly women, helped me in this endeavor. I worked in the same room as George, watched the reporters come and go, and listened to George's rap on Lyndon. I ferried press releases to the Senate Press Gallery and soon came to know some of the reporters superficially. I found myself deeply attracted to one specific man, a *Time* reporter about ten years older than me. He was unlike the Texas men I had known—and he was married. It was intoxicating to sit in the Senate Gallery and flirt across the Senate floor while he was in the Press Gallery covering the goings-on. This was heady stuff for a twenty-five-year-old girl from McAllen.

THE LBJ CHARISMA

LBJ obligated those around him. In some cases he made them rich, and they felt indebted; in others, his powerful personality and political clout acted as a deterrent to any negative action or talk. Everyone knew Johnson could do serious harm if he took a notion to do so, so they remained loyal to the point of being in denial about some of his bad behavior, even though it was obvious. Like abused children, some of Johnson's old staffers have gone through life sucking up to the LBJ legend and its remnants, basking in the reflected glory and never acknowledging the less-savory parts of his complicated personality.

Johnson did us some very nice favors, but I found these situations uncomfortable—I didn't want to be obligated too. At one point he told Billy Lee to let him know when he wanted to buy a car, the implication being that he could get a good deal for us. I feel sure that this was a well-meaning gesture, but it was a favor nevertheless. Favors obligated employees to sing LBJ's praises, without talking about his darker side. He was a consummate manipulator; we were learning at the feet of the master.

Still, in spite of LBJ's culpabilities, and even though we considered him a bully, Bill and I were proud to be working for this forceful, powerful majority leader, with his larger-than-life image, and we defended his actions to our liberal friends in Texas. We were fascinated by him, and by Washington and politics in general. There was so much going on; it was stimulating and exhilarating. Lyndon worked all the time—he was everywhere, giving orders to everyone, all the time. He and Lady Bird were upscaling; he sent her to Elizabeth Arden to improve her looks. He took an active interest in the appearance of his secretaries, especially the ones who worked directly with him. He wore custom-made suits that camouflaged his long torso and big belly. He and "Bird," as he called his wife, were rich enough at this point to have a nice, comfortable home in northwest Washington, across the street from J. Edgar Hoover's house. They flew back and forth from Washington to Texas in planes owned by corporations like Brown & Root, which at that time was a Texas construction company. George Brown and his brother Herman had underwritten LBJ for years and the favors were returned in kind. Staff members knew when there was a flight going to or from Texas and hitched rides if there was room.

Bill and I started work for Lyndon just as he was entering the national consciousness. He wasn't on the general public's radar yet, but the big boys on Wall Street, in labor, and in business were beginning to take notice. Much of the gossip on the Hill and the political conversation among our friends involved how well LBJ was doing in his quest to woo the national press and the northeastern financial community.

So immersed were we in the minutiae of our jobs that we often had no idea exactly what LBJ was doing until we read it in the press. At the point that we arrived in Washington in 1955 Johnson was being criticized for his one-man rule of the Senate in his role as majority leader. He was moving left in order to position himself as a more mainstream Democrat for a national ticket, all the while assuring Texas conservatives that he was not a liberal.

During 1955 and 1956, Bill and I spent quite a bit of time with LBJ at his home in D.C., as well as several weekends in Middleburg,

Virginia, at George Brown's (of Brown & Root) pre–Civil War mansion with LBJ and Frank "Posh" Oltorf, who was Brown's lobbyist. A behind-the-scenes political insider, Oltorf often socialized with staffers he particularly liked, and our friendship resulted in more exposure to Johnson than we would've had otherwise. Bill and I wanted to spend time with Sidney and Shelby on weekends, but if The Senator called, we felt we had to respond. It wasn't easy to say no to Lyndon.

I admired Johnson for his stand on censuring Joe McCarthy and insisting on civil rights legislation. My hope was that he was a closet liberal who only moved in the conservative money circles to get elected. Bill and I made this point to our liberal Texas friends when they claimed that LBJ was a duplicitous opportunist, and they would grudgingly quiet down.

Sam Rayburn was the powerful Speaker of the House, and a close ally of Johnson's. A smart, seasoned politician who both admired and felt a deep affection for Lyndon, he lived and breathed the Congress. Mr. Rayburn frequently visited Lyndon's offices on the Senate side. The shoulders of his suit bore a constant dusting of dandruff; I was always tempted to brush it away. The secretaries liked Rayburn because he was endearing and nonthreatening—he always remembered us and cracked jokes about Congress ("The Committee on Foreign Affairs is so named in the House and the Committee on Foreign Relations is so named in the Senate because by the time a member of the House gets to the Senate, he is too old to have anything but 'relations'").

In July, Johnson suffered what was deemed a "moderately severe" heart attack while at Brown's home in Middleburg. He was hospitalized in D.C. for five weeks and then convalesced at his ranch in Texas until December. Many speculated that his illness might remove him from consideration for the Democratic presidential nomination, which most assumed would go to Adlai Stevenson. But Johnson quit his several-packs-a-day smoking habit, modified his voracious diet (before the heart attack he would often pull the serving bowls close for better access), cut out caffeine, and began to swim in his newly built pool at the ranch. Hard candies were kept available to relieve his acute urge to smoke.

Johnson operated out of the LBJ ranch near Johnson City for the next several months. A steady stream of visitors flowed to his side: colleagues, politicians, friends, relatives, staff, and, eventually, members of the press. Lyndon's convalescence in Texas provided an opportunity to visit with key players in the state Democratic Party factions, devise strategies, and get a feel for how to unify the party in time for the 1956 convention—at the time, the Texas Democratic Party was split between the Shivercrats, supporters of the very conservative Governor Allan Shivers, and the more moderate Democrats, who supported LBJ. Delivering the Texas delegation to the Democrats would reflect well on Johnson's state and national leadership abilities.

There were several female staff members in their thirties and forties who had worked for him for years in Washington; they were now ensconced on the second floor of the ranch house. Since LBJ worked such long days—all the while touting to the public his newfound dedication to rest and recovery—they worked in shifts. My perception is that they were extraordinarily loyal, but I can only imagine how they all fared in close quarters. Lady Bird certainly had her hands full.

Then, in September of 1956, President Eisenhower had his own heart attack. It was more serious than Johnson's, but eventually both men fully recovered. Neither the Republicans nor the Democrats would be able to play the health card in the upcoming presidential election. To highlight his complete recovery and cement his legislative agenda, Johnson came up with his "Program with a Heart," unveiled in a speech in Whitney, Texas. "Program with a Heart" consisted of thirteen proposals that LBJ would submit to the Democratic Policy Committee, including a bill to broaden Social Security, a tax revision benefiting low-income groups, a program to aid medical research (apparently the heart attack had gotten his attention on the health care issue), and, buried in the middle, a natural gas bill that would appease Johnson's financial backers in Texas.

Speaker of the House Rayburn spent a lot of time plotting and planning with The Senator. They were a potent team. Rayburn released a statement to the press saying simply that Texas's political situation could be solved by making Lyndon the "favorite son" and chairman of the Texas delegation to the Democratic National Convention.

THE 1956 ELECTION

When Congress convened in January of 1956, President Eisenhower and Majority Leader Johnson were back at their respective posts in the White House and on the Senate floor. Lyndon looked healthy. He had lost a great deal of weight and was once again running at full tilt. His desire for the presidency hadn't waned; he was energetic and reinvigorated. And 1956 was going to be a big year for politics.

The Texas Democratic Party, split between the conservative Shivercrats and LBJ's more moderate supporters, became the backdrop for a power struggle between Governor Shivers and Senator Johnson. Shivers said he wouldn't support LBJ for the presidential nomination if LBJ were supported by the Democratic Advisory Council, the liberal faction of the Texas Democratic Party. Shivers was a slick, darkly handsome, gentlemanly type who was used to the good life. He grew up poor but married Mary Alice Shary, a very rich woman from Mission, Texas. Johnson, on the other hand, was the country version of Sammy Glick, the ethically challenged and driven protagonist of Budd Schulberg's novel, *What Makes Sammy Run?*, getting there by any means. Eventually LBJ accused Shivers of plotting to destroy the Texas Democratic Party. And Shivers didn't have the benefits of a well-oiled public relations machine on Capitol Hill. Texas was blanketed with "you are my friend, my friend" letters; we staffers manned robotypers—odd-looking machines that reproduced letters—around the clock. Sometimes Bill and I were called into work in the middle of the night to run the dreaded machines.

The Harris-Fulbright Bill of 1956, which exempted natural gas producers from federal regulation, was eventually cleared for consideration by the Senate, after much finagling by LBJ. President Eisenhower then vetoed it after Senator Francis Case of South Dakota blew the whistle on a couple of Texas lobbyists whom Case charged with attempted bribery. It was all very unseemly, and a perfect reason to veto the bill. But Lyndon had done his job by getting it passed, so he couldn't be blamed for the bill's downfall.

The Senator was also watching as racial segregation began to split the country in two. White bigots in the South were trying to maintain the status quo with intimidation, humiliation, and violence, while southern congressmen were trying to do the same via the Southern Manifesto, which attempted to reverse the 1954 United States Supreme Court's *Brown v. Board of Education* desegregation ruling. One hundred and one southern congressmen signed it in March of 1956. Lyndon did not sign, and I was proud of him for it.

Johnson's position as chairman and favorite son of the Texas Democratic delegation to the 1956 Democratic National Convention was a good cover for his real fight for the presidential nomination—he needed to avoid raising the awareness of the liberals who opposed him. Questionnaires were sent to the constituents from a group of Johnson's southern colleagues in the Senate asking for feedback about his support. Americans for Democratic Action (ADA) said they couldn't support Johnson because of his conservatism and questionable civil rights record; this played well to the conservatives in Texas. Meanwhile, the AFL-CIO endorsed him; this looked good to liberals.

All of these actions had been engineered by Lyndon, whose eye by now was even more firmly focused on a future in the White House, whenever that might be. Johnson was interacting at all levels of government, working the phones, talking with district and precinct supporters, and leading the Senate. George Reedy, his national pressman, thought ahead and fed memos to The Senator regarding national issues on which he could comment, in an effort to prove to the nation that Johnson wasn't simply a regional politico.

The way things fell out, however, meant that 1956 was not destined to be Johnson's year. The Republican Eisenhower-Nixon ticket was in place, and it looked like Adlai Stevenson would once again receive the Democratic nomination for president. Down in Texas, Governor Shivers was cranky about Johnson being selected chairman and favorite son of the Texas delegation, so he announced that he wouldn't support a Stevenson-Johnson ticket. At the convention in Chicago, there was a heap of horse trade and chatter about balancing the Democratic ticket with a Southerner as VP, i.e., Johnson. But for all the speculation that LBJ was a perfect vice presidential candidate, he declined to be considered for the post, to the confusion and consternation of many. Senator Estes Kefauver of Tennessee was chosen instead. Apparently Johnson was fixed on winning the top office or nothing.

Back home in Texas, Senator Price Daniel, a conservative, defeated Ralph Yarborough, a liberal, in the runoff for governor. LBJ, Lady Bird, and various state politicos and politicas toured the state campaigning for the national Democratic ticket, but were criticized for not mentioning Stevenson and Kefauver prominently enough in their speeches. On November 6, 1956, Eisenhower and Nixon defeated Stevenson and Kefauver. By this time, the liberal Kefauver was perceived as a fool in a coonskin cap who wasn't a big enough draw for Stevenson. Texas liberals were incensed because they didn't think that LBJ had pushed hard enough for the national ticket, but the conservatives were thrilled.

For Lyndon, the 1956 election was a dress rehearsal that would prove beneficial in the future. He was now in good shape in Texas. He continued on course, attending a NATO conference in Paris in November, just after the convention. Lady Bird went along, and they took a well-deserved side trip to Germany. (Later in my life, when I was a congressional wife, I learned that it is extremely hard work to be married to a politician if one or both of you is as ambitious as Lyndon and Lady Bird were. Like her husband, Lady Bird worked constantly. Effective political wives are much like first-rate executives. She took care of business, even while she was waiting for her children at the dentist's office. She fed visitors well and was always pleasant and organized. She hardly ever visited the Senate office, and I remember the staff feeling a bit self-conscious when she was present. Later, during my years as a political wife, I did as Lady Bird had done. I rarely spent time in my husband's office—I wanted to keep his staff as allies.) After all they had been through in 1955 and 1956, Lady Bird and Lyndon needed that trip to Paris.

And Bill and I deserved our first vacation to New York City. We drove there with our friends, Cile Ragland, who worked for Congressman Homer Thornberry of Austin, and her boyfriend, Norman Fischer, a D.C. native. We drove there in Norman's 1956 black convertible with red interior. *My Fair Lady* had just opened on Broadway; we had been playing the album for weeks. The city was magical at that time. We hooked up with friends who lived there, and my memories of the trip are in black and white, just like the fifties movies. We had no problem parking on the street in Midtown, and we walked and wandered and ate in restaurants in the West Village. I was enormously stimulated by the city and yearned to someday make it my home.

A MARRIAGE ON THE VERGE

I was trying my hardest to be a straight wife, but I longed for that *Time* reporter. Eventually our mutual desire brought us together in a hotel room. The sex was great; I felt simultaneously guilty and exhilarated. I had fantasies of leaving Bill, but I continued trying to be a good mother, to keep my life with Bill and the children together, and to be an effective employee for The Senator. I was conflicted and, I realize now, somewhat depressed. I tried going to a psychologist with the hope that he would "fix" me and turn me into a "good wife," but unbeknownst to me, the psychologist contacted Bill and had a session with *him*. I felt conspired against. Then, during the latter part of 1956, I found out that I was pregnant again.

I was facing bringing up three children with a husband who still hadn't gained control of his financial habits. He collected Brooks Brothers suits and continued buying items on credit. He had neglected to make the payments on the little house we bought in Austin, and we had lost it. I was anxious about money and knew I would have to continue to work to pay the bills that Bill incurred. He was spending time in Texas with The Senator, and I was relieved to have some time to sort out my feelings. I considered having an abortion.

Bill reported back from Austin about the great parties, the back-roads tours, the new people he'd met, and his fling with an Austin girl. All of this saddened me; I was utterly confused about my marriage and had the usual pregnancy sickness, but I didn't have the guts to tell Bill about it over the phone. I couldn't bring myself to voice what I wanted to say: "I want out of this situation. I don't want to be a mother of three in Washington, D.C., who has to work an office job *and* run the household. And I especially hate being away from my kids all the time." I gave up on Bill ever controlling his profligacy, but the thought of being divorced and trying to support two, much less three, children in addition to myself was frightening enough to stop me from airing my true feelings.

Bill arrived home before I could get an abortion. He insisted that he wanted to stay married and have another child. He knew his spending habits were destructive, and he reiterated that he needed to make more money so I could stay at home with the children. We both carried guilt about our respective flings, but we vowed to stay together and stay with LBJ. Bill voiced his hopes of one day getting a novel published, and he honestly believed that its publication would make everyone happy and solve all our problems. After this near-catastrophe, our marriage improved somewhat. The crisis jolted us into a new sort of intimacy; our little girls were precious to us, and we wanted to work it out for them. In order to distance myself from the *Time* reporter, I requested a transfer to the office where Johnson's Texas press people, Booth Mooney and Bill Brammer, were ensconced.

Bill was miserable, because he knew I longed for another man, and I felt a lot of guilt. In spite of this, Bill, Booth, and I had a great time in the huge Democratic Policy Conference Room in the Senate Office Building, which served as our office, located just under Vice President Nixon's office. It had a massive conference table and an oversized leather couch. Bill acquired a Telefunken stereo for the office and voilà, we had our salon. We entertained friends by letting them eavesdrop on the vice president's commode flushing overhead; I listened to music while scanning the Texas newspapers and clipping items I thought The Senator should see. Our setup was interrupted every so often by delegations from Texas, for whom Lady Bird would stop by with Texas-shaped cookies. LBJ was impressive and direct in those closed-door receptions. To a group of farmers whining about how the government was making them comply with housing standards for immigrant farm workers (like requiring windows, for instance), he verbally grabbed them by the lapels, saying, "You gotta *give* something to *get* something."

Despite LBJ's crudeness, tantrums, and adulterous, lecherous ways—although, let's be honest, who was I to point a finger?—I still liked him. I'd slip into the Senate Gallery and watch him on the Senate floor, moving about, talking softly, running the place. His grasp of the rules was amazing. Bobby Baker, the young secretary to the Senate majority leader, murmured constantly in LBJ's ear. He was perfect for the job; we joked that his head grew off his body at an angle so he could more conveniently whisper into the majority leader's ear. I felt proud of The Senator as I watched him in action, but then I would catch him doing something like using a paper clip to dig in his ear or pulling a sheet of paper off his desk to floss, slipping it between his teeth. This on the Senate floor!

Around this time, Bill began to write the novel he had always talked about. This early effort eventually evolved into *The Gay Place,* a trilogy of political novellas that would come to hold an exalted place in the canon of Texas literature. From the beginning, I had believed in Bill's talent and never doubted that he would be a published writer.

Our schedule was odd and exhausting. After dinner, we put the girls to bed and Bill took a nap until midnight, when he got up to write. Sometime between midnight and 7 a.m., I would wake up, read what he had written, and we'd discuss it. Bill had begun taking Dexedrine, the speed drug of the fifties, which doctors freely prescribed. I knew he liked drugs that kept him awake; when we were first married, we took Benzedrine, which we bought in Mexico. I probably would've ended up a speed freak but for the fact that my body didn't like the drug, but Bill didn't have this problem. He took any kind of speed he could find, popping pills continuously, staying up for days to write. Of course, at that point we didn't know how adversely speed affected our bodies—after all, doctors prescribed it.

We continued observing the goings-on in the political world with deep interest, entertaining friends in our office since we had a lot of space and privacy far away from the rest of the LBJ offices. From the window we watched a deeply tanned Jack Kennedy get out of his limousine, marveling at his beauty and confidence as he strode into the building. Kennedy and LBJ were allies; they were both garnering greater and greater power. But some of the more liberal senators were growing restless with Lyndon's leadership. Lyndon knew where the political center was, but he knew it was an unstable place to be—the political spectrum is organic, constantly shifting as the populace shifts. Johnson's goal was to control the Senate and hold on to his position.

Bill was excelling in his job, observing the relationships of the staff and studying The Senator constantly. He was more enamored of Johnson than I ever was—I was forced to keep emotional and physical distance in an effort to prevent unwanted sexual advances. But I liked LBJ very much, and The Senator knew it.

DEEP IN THE HEART

It had been two years since I'd been back to Texas, and I was desperate to see the Texas sky and feel the sun burn my skin and warm my bones. My parents had missed out on seeing our little girls for too long. Although I enjoyed working in the Senate and knew I could advance in Lyndon's organization, children came first. Anticipating being a mother of three had me yearning for Austin, where life was easier, cheaper, and healthier. Maintaining homes in both D.C. and Austin seemed financially impossible, but I insisted on it.

I wrote a carefully worded note to LBJ saying that only motherhood could take me away from him. The nurturing women on the staff arranged a party for my departure, which was held in Lyndon's elegant majority leader's suite. Lyndon put his arm around me and said, "If you'll name that boy after me, I'll give him a heifer calf and he'll have a whole herd by the time he's twenty-one."

As my little girls and I flew back to Texas (this time on a commercial plane), I was hugely pregnant and happy to be returning to wide-open skies and life in Austin. (I thought I was through with Washington, but what I couldn't have known then was that Lyndon Johnson would be a constant in my life— sometimes peripherally, sometimes centrally—until his death.) Bill and I had both been changed by working for LBJ. He taught us that both sides of an issue had to be weighed with the public interest in mind. He had little patience with extreme liberals or extreme conservatives, but he would work with both types, and he was usually successful in making them see his point of view. He spoke to us quietly, like a teacher, often dropping in one of his homilies: "Never trust a nary-assed man," "You ain't learning anything when you're talking," and "Your judgment is only as good as your information" are just three of many.

On May 24, 1957, our son, Willie, named after our favorite journalist, Willie Morris, was born. Soon afterward, Lyndon and Bill both happened to be in Austin, and The Senator asked Bill to fly with him and Mary Margaret Wiley, his number one secretary, to Washington over the weekend to tend to an errand. Bill was home so seldom that he didn't want to go, but I needed a break from child-rearing, so I called Lyndon and suggested that I go in Bill's stead. The next day the three of us boarded an oil company plane (which, unfortunately, was not as comfortably pressurized as the Brown & Root planes) bound for D.C. We drank Scotch, of course, and Mary Margaret and I defended our liberal friends. Lyndon couldn't let it rest. He didn't like Ronnie Dugger, the editor of the *Texas Observer,* worth a damn. When his arguments failed to bring us around, he resorted to saying, "If you look back far enough in his [Ronnie's] family, you'll find a dwarf." For his part, Ronnie didn't like him either.

We passed a pleasant weekend in Johnson's Washington home. Lady Bird was not there. The Senator tended to business between Scotches and gossiping and trying to get his two young companions to see things his way. He kept his hands to himself, seeming much more relaxed; I felt warmly toward him. Mary Margaret called the shots. She knew Johnson better than anyone. The younger members of LBJ's entourage considered her a good influence because she was "one of us," a younger, hipper staffer who prodded him to the left. And even though he was playing the political game just right by sending one message to the liberals and another to the conservatives, we were impatient and wanted more results.

Back in Austin, our politically conscious friends were obsessed with LBJ, wanting to know whether he was truly liberal or simply conservative. Was he as crude as they'd heard? They all wanted to meet him. I loved living with my children in the big, old, comfortable house on Enfield Road that Bill had rented and I had fixed up before Willie was born. A beautiful young Mexican-Irish girl came to live with me and look after the children in exchange for room and board. She had many brothers and sisters, so she was great with the kids. When she arrived after school, I went out with my friends. When Bill was home, we partied together, and when Lyndon was at the ranch, we spent weekends out there, including the children.

Lyndon and Lady Bird had created a Texas spread with all the comforts—all of their houses, in fact, were warm, accommodating, and without pretension. Lyndon was relaxed during this period. One day I was driving in the vicinity of the ranch with several friends and we decided to drop by, unannounced. We came upon

Lyndon floating around in his swimming pool, happy to see us, with Wayne King blasting from speakers hung in trees.

Weekends at the ranch were much the same as those in Washington, but the atmosphere was far more relaxed. Lyndon held forth, telling stories and laughing, surrounded by staff, Jessie Kellum (his radio/TV station manager), Donald Thomas (his lawyer), and local cronies. We drank, ate, and gathered around him, listening and getting assignments for whatever it was he wanted. Lyndon soaked up the attention while Lady Bird saw to it that everyone had a drink and was comfortable. Zephyr Wright, the Johnsons' black cook, churned out popovers and bowls of 1950s food served family style.

Lady Bird always seemed busy and preoccupied—the same criticism voiced by my children later, when I was a congressional wife. At the time Bill and I were too young to appreciate Lady Bird's importance; I think that's why Bill gave her short shrift as Sweet Mama in *The Gay Place.* He didn't understand how crucial she was to enabling Lyndon's power—and neither did I, until I was a congressional wife. After observing The Senator's behavior with female staff members and women in general, I often wondered how Lady Bird put up with him. His womanizing was obvious. He would holler "BIRD!" if he wanted her attention, and like magic she would appear. He sometimes humiliated her in front of other people. But Lady Bird was of another generation, wise enough not to respond to his crudeness. She was willing to ignore his behavior, for she was secure in her position as his wife, and he needed her and loved her in his way. Also, she desired power just as much as he did. Theirs was a creative relationship that served to accomplish their mutual goals for money and political power. She had to either compromise and put up with the guy, or leave—so she compromised. I think Lady Bird was a superb First Lady. When Lyndon died, she inherited the money and prestige of everything they had built, all of which she richly deserved. When she spoke, it came from a very high place.

During this time, 1957–1958, Bill was living in a basement room in the Betty Alden Inn, because it was cheap and near the office. He hated it. He was working on his novel at night and bemoaning our separation. Although Bill and I both acknowledged that Austin was the best place to raise our children, living separately was eroding our marriage. I felt the sting of the separation too, but the thought of moving back to Washington with three children was unthinkable. There was one good thing that came out of this difficult time, however: Bill's loneliness, his living space, and his liberal use of amphetamines imposed a discipline of sorts, and he finished work on the manuscript that became *The Gay Place.*

Bill's letters reflected his sadness, but at the same time, he was having a very interesting life. He traveled to New York City frequently. He also spent time with LBJ at George Brown's place. His letter of February 3, 1958, describes the scene:

> Left here about 3:00 Saturday in the limousine. Jenkins, Thornberrys, LBJs, and Mary Margaret and me. It was a lot of fun. The Virginia country was beautiful after the snow. We got there about 5, immediately started drinking, had people waiting on us hand and foot, had a sumptuous meal. Everybody turned in about 8 but I stayed up until midnight watching TV, playing records, reading books. Also there was George [Brown's] or Herman's adopted daughter, I don't know which, and a friend of hers, both Smith girls, very intelligent and liberal. They were holidaying. Same routine Sunday, more drinking (milk punch in the morning), storytelling, very pleasant, no LBJ scenes, everybody relaxed and beautiful. Another enormous meal, with servants hovering all over. Best story: LBJ talking about Shivers, about last year after their fight. Shivers called him one day just to "pay respects." LBJ invited him to hotel room in Austin for a drink. Shivers said Bill Francis is here, invited him over for a drink to his hotel room instead. Said they sat there from 3 in afternoon until midnight, "Allan with a fifth of bourbon and me with a fifth of Scotch . . . Bill Francis passed out about sundown; we sat there throwing lances at each other, dodging,

> jumping like stuck pigs when we was hit. Finally carried Bill Francis out into the limousine at midnight." LBJ said: "I guess we understand each other." Somebody said, "He used to love the people," and LBJ said "Yes, but doesn't anymore." LBJ waved his arm about the room and said, "Here's how you forget. You sit here at a big dining table before a crackling fire and carpets three inches thick. Now tell me. Are you very worked up about the suffering in the world at this moment? That's what you got to watch out for." That man!

"That man" would be elected vice president of the United States in just two short years.

THE BEST OF TIMES, THE WORST OF TIMES

From Bill, dated June 4, 1958:

> Dear Mama:
>
> Am finally coming out of my post-novel hypnosis and functioning again. Trouble is, all I think about now is getting home to you and kiddies. I finished the book Sunday 10 a.m. after working all night Saturday night and into the morning. The Memorial Day weekend gave me a lot of time. I worked all night Thursday night, all night Friday night after sleeping most of the day, and then Saturday night and into Sunday. My last four chapters were colossal. I edited the thing lightly Monday and shipped it off to Street [Bill's literary agent] yesterday. It will be interesting to see his reaction. Will send you the carbon as soon as I find out whether I will need it for rewriting purposes.
>
> This is a pay-the-bills day, and all I can do is try to plug the gaps and pray that the pay raise bill trickles down to LBJ's staff. It will be a 10 percent increase—about $40 or $50 a month for me after taxes. Hope we make it through the summer until I can get back to Austin. Have just about decided I may have to stay on LBJ's staff for a few months after the session ends so we can

save enough money for the move back to Washington. If you want to move. It breaks my heart to think of pulling Sidney out of her nice school. Maybe I'll get the book published; maybe we'll make a lot of money; perhaps they'll take me off to jail.

You sounded "down" when I talked with you Saturday. Was it a hangover from the Maco party? Wish I had been there. It is miserable here, and it seems worse when I think of having to live with these people for another year. David and Harry maintain it is much better here; I think they are mad.

Good Bernie called yesterday evening and gave me the only happy evening since you left. We went to Chez Odet and had a cheap French dinner, with wine and snails and the works. He and I are so homosexual together. He says you are beautiful and hello. After dinner we went to his place and the McPhersons and Nicholsons and David came by and it was all so goddam shrill I wanted to catch a plane to Texas.

Will write again when I am in a better mood or when Street responds. Tell S & S hello for me; miss all of you hideously. A thousand kisses! (I have been reading Flaubert's letters)

b

And then, soon after:

Wednesday

. . . The trip back was uneventful. LBJ had about sixteen Scotches but did not get drunk and never went to sleep. He talked all the way and was in high spirits. He kept talking about me going to work in the Valley, and all I could offer was a sick smile. . . .

A letter from Street was awaiting me when I got back. He is always full of bad news. He said: "I am as lost as you about what to do with the book . . . I think the key problem is that the story is just too morbid. Jay deserves better than he receives, and without making him a character with whom the reader can identify, you lose a foil. You must have a healthy background against which you can operate your characters, and that ain't here.

> It would be a disservice to you to submit it as is, but I hesitate to ask you to go back and work on it until you have had time to think about it . . ."
>
> I don't want to think about it. I couldn't possibly write it non-morbid with a "healthy" background. I don't think Street and I are on the same vibrations. If he had made any other kind of criticism, I could feel much better—anything about style, construction, etc. But how he can refuse to submit this and be so goddam enthusiastic about the first book (which was certainly inferior to the second) is beyond me. [*The Gay Place* consists of three separate, but related, novellas.] What do you think? I think I will say to hell with it and send it to Harry's friend who runs the pocket books thing. I don't mind working on it, but it would be impossible to write it "healthy."
>
> Anyhow, I am starting another book this week—another short one—just to get my mind off this publishing madness. Idiot agents make me morbid.

By the end of 1958, Bill had become progressively more unhappy, complaining about our living arrangement and lack of money. But, at the same time, his productivity on *The Gay Place* had paid off: after much back-and-forth, his agent had passed the manuscript on to an editor at Houghton Mifflin. This was encouraging.

While waiting for an answer from Houghton Mifflin (to which he referred, with his typical wit, as "Houston Muffin"), Bill spent time in New York City with Eliot and Elizabeth Janeway, enjoying the literary atmosphere. When Houghton Mifflin decided to publish *The Gay Place*, Bill felt he finally had the latitude to make some new choices, so he went to work for Eliot Janeway, an economist, political operator, and supporter of Johnson's who published an economic newsletter in New York City. Janeway was lining up money and delegates for Lyndon's second bid for the presidency in 1960. A friendship had developed between Bill and Michael Janeway, Eliot's older son, who had been a summer intern for Johnson. Bill was fascinated by this smart, well-educated young man, whose mother was the novelist Elizabeth Janeway. The Janeway family was very nurturing to Bill, but he wasn't happy with the job. From a letter during this period:

> My feeling this week is no feeling, or rather the absence of feeling. Probably as a result of being so high for so long. Am not down, but sort of out. Finishing the book, getting the response from the publisher, coming to terms with something or other, going to Texas, coming back and feeling glorious in my new Brooks Bros. suit—too bad I couldn't be bubbly the rest of the year. And all the reasons were so shitty superficial, or ephemeral, or something. . . . The morning I got back from Texas I was still high and performed well for LBJ. There was a staff meeting called that I hadn't known about and I was included and they could hardly shut me up. LB was impressed, but I can't, at this point, remember a single thing I said. LBJ is like a shot of adrenalin; his personal magic lasts just about as long, though. . . . Am going home; office shut down; dark outside; guard offering me beer for use of the couch. What grim slobs they all are around here.

SADNESS PERMEATED THE MARRIAGE

Bill briefly went to Los Angeles to work with LBJ delegates, and then returned to Texas to work for the Johnson campaign two months before the election. His appendix ruptured, and he was in the hospital for a few days. Eventually he moved into a small apartment adjoining the house where the children and I were living in Austin. Although we lived at the same address, we were separated.

Meanwhile, I had been working in the 1959 session of the Texas Legislature, partying and living it up in Austin à la *The Gay Place,* taking care of the children and avoiding dealing with my (almost) moribund marriage with Bill. These were some of the best and worst of times for me. It was a heady time, and I was having fun, but there were moments when the familiarity of guilt and the reality of our situation took over. I filled my life with children, working, socializing, and trying not to think about the future, which helped avoid some of the pain.

I developed close relationships with other young mothers my age who were also in damaged marriages, either waiting for divorce settlements or running from their situations by having affairs. Figuring out where to meet in the evening or which party to attend was a main concern of the day. Phone lines were busy around 5 p.m. The mix of friends in Austin at that time brought together professors like John Sullivan and musicians like the Modern Jazz Quartet (who weren't allowed to stay in our all-white hotels even though they were highly renowned and influential jazz artists). We loved showing visiting celebrities the Texas Hill Country's unbelievably beautiful places to picnic and swim, the hot dry hills contrasting with cool pools of spring water falling through limestone strata. We often wound up at Pat and Mike Levi's Paleface Ranch on the Pedernales River, where we sat atop the hill and watched the landscape spread out before us in the orange light of the setting sun. We drank and listened to Errol Garner or Sinatra while Pat and Mike prepared simple but elegant dinners of thick steaks, salad, potatoes, and wine.

Working in the Texas legislature turned out to be more fun than I had anticipated. Watching "the lege" in action was fascinating. At that point secretaries could sit beside their members on the House floor and watch the proceedings while the House was in session. The Texas legislature is not known for being a great deliberative body, and at that time it was more like one big party.

I tried to merely observe and stay detached, but I soon became smitten with one of the legislators, a representative from Dallas. We weren't discreet, and we were both married. We partied with my friends, who soon became his friends, spending many afternoons on his boat on Town Lake and some weekends with the Levis at Paleface. The affair was very romantic while it lasted, full of good times, great fifties music, long good-byes, and wonderful dinners. Our time together was charged with sexual anticipation and romance.

When Bill learned of the affair, he was not pleased, even though we were separated and he was having affairs as well. He declared that he was going to Dallas to confront the legislator about our behavior. Upon his return, I asked him how it went. Bill said, "He's terrific. I think I'll divorce you and marry him." Bob Hughes, that legislator, became the role model for Roy Sherwood in *The Gay Place.* I continued to see Bob sporadically, but after a while it became obvious that he wasn't going to leave his wife and the relationship eventually died from lack of energy and the long distance between us.

The Gay Place, on the other hand, was just coming to life. In January of 1959, Houghton Mifflin bit and Bill received a publishing contract and a $1,500 advance. But in spite of this success, we would never realize Bill's dream that our marriage would work itself out and we'd live happily ever after. By the time he called with the good news about *The Gay Place*, I was already far away, both emotionally and physically, and enjoying myself in the Austin mode.

A NOVEL FINDS SUCCESS, BUT A MARRIAGE CRUMBLES

The Gay Place hit bookstores in 1961, two months after John Kennedy and Lyndon Johnson became president and vice president. Figuring out the real-life counterparts to the characters in *The Gay Place* became a preoccupation in Austin. I immediately recognized everyone among our friends. I believed that Bill had used my affair with Bob Hughes for the Roy Sherwood character, who was part of the fabric of the complicated plot of *The Flea Circus*, a novella about the loss of love, aspirations to power, and betrayal, and I felt exploited. *The Flea Circus* is full of young bright people who are obsessed with partying and intent on avoiding their personal problems (sound familiar?). At the center of the plot is an LBJ-like governor who manipulates young legislators, playing both sides and employing questionable means in the pursuit of worthwhile ends.

The book was an instant literary success. Bill was ecstatic. His self-confidence grew; women began to come after him in earnest.

I, on the other hand, felt somewhat used after reading the book. It was similar to the feeling that would come over me when Bill had quizzed me about my conversations with men at parties. I didn't want to be married to Bill anymore, and was exhausted by my continuing ambivalence. In fact, I was exhausted by a lot of things. Finally, I felt, the marriage had worn itself out.

I spoke to John Osorio, a lawyer and friend I had met through the Levis, about getting a divorce. I was hesitant about it, because I knew it would be difficult to support three children by myself—although Bill loved his kids, his history with money didn't bode well for our future financial stability. But I asked John to go ahead and file, because I felt I had to get on with my life, no matter what may lie ahead. Though a critical success, *The Gay Place* had not been a commercial success, so there really wasn't any community property. Osorio got Bill to waive his rights to *The Gay Place*, assigning half to me and half to our children. (These rights were all Bill had. I didn't even realize that I myself had been granted half of *The Gay Place* until years later—at the time, I just wanted out of the marriage, and I only glanced at the fine print.) Before the divorce was final, I found a small house half a block from Sidney and Shelby's school for $11,500. I called Bill, who by then had begun working for *Time* in Atlanta, and told him that I needed down payment money for a home for our children—a large down payment was necessary because Bill's spending habits had wreaked havoc with our credit rating. He sent the money, and we moved into the house immediately. The little house was perfect for the four of us, leaving me incredibly relieved. Bill showed up every once in a while to see the kids. The divorce was finalized in June of 1961, and the judge set child support at $300 per month.

BILL'S SWINGING SIXTIES

With Kennedy and Johnson in the White House, there was an air of hopefulness in the country. Kennedy inspired us to excel. And as the vice president, he had can-do Lyndon, who knew how to get things done in the Senate, backing him up. Jackie, who had style, inspired us to wear little shift dresses and tease our hair into bouffant flips.

Bill and I were living in parallel universes. *The Gay Place* had won the 1961 Houghton Mifflin Literary Fellowship, granting Bill a $10,000 award. ("It's a big deal . . . Houghton Mifflin's biggest. They award only one fellowship a year—and some years they skip it entirely if they feel there's no book deserving it. . . . Sort of singles one out from being just another clod author," Bill wrote.) He was enjoying his time in the sun as a "famous arthur." During his tenure at *Time* he connected with Diana de Vegh, an actress and one of the many women President Kennedy sneaked into his Georgetown house while Jackie was ensconced in the West Wing of the White House. Bill told me that he had been at Diana's when JFK called. She was in the shower, so Bill answered the phone. Kennedy asked, "Is Diana theah?" Bill said he was tempted to say, "No, she's gone to Cuber."

Years later, in 1973, Diana de Vegh let Bill move into her apartment on Central Park West. Shelby and I, in New York City for the weekend, visited with Bill and Al Reinert at Diana's. She was hospitable and kind enough to invite us to lunch. She had set a lovely table with wine goblets; Bill sat at the head of the table and filled his with his beloved Dr. Pepper.

Bill's social circles overlapped with those of the Kennedy-Johnson presidency circle. At the time he wrote this letter, on July 21, 1961, he was still working for *Time*:

> I am white-white as can be. Thought I would be turned a gorgeous Man-Tan hue last weekend because, after my coup (with official, extremely rare and favorable whoops from the NY editors) with Katherine Anne Porter, choicest assignment—an aeroplane jaunt with the Prez to Hiatus Port. They thought they were doing me a favor. I was hoping to pursue Ayub (or Cong. Abe Kahn of the Bronx, as M. Janeway calls him) and LBJ to Texas. Anyhow, I missed out on the cooney fetes at Johnson City, and

> instead went to Cape Cod, where for four days we experienced every sort of weather but the good sort: rain, hail, wind, fog, cold (55 degrees). It was what the Cape Cod resort town newspapers describe as "inclement." I returned to D.C. on Tuesday sporting a color suggestive of Mai Britt's underarm, eyes smarting from 80 hours of poker in a motel room filled with Pierre Salinger Corona-Carona fumes. I felt close to history, but such self-induced therapeutic comfortings rarely sustain one beyond the time it takes to endure one round of drinks with a group of mucky-eyed journalists and a pair of twice-divorced "dancing studio" instructors from Cincinnati (under questioning from these last two, I admitted to being in the chorus of the Chocolate Soldier operetta which was playing that weekend at the local summer stock tent show; last day there they were still bugging me for tickets, remarking on my beautiful legs, and insisting that they had recognized me as a "dancer" even before they had been so informed).

In contrast to Bill's, my life with the children in our small two-bedroom house was more settled. I knew that Bill and his friends were taking drugs, so I didn't let the kids spend the night at his place, where there was constant partying. (Alcohol was still the drug of choice for me and my fellow hypocrites.) I got up at 5 a.m. to exercise, make breakfast, and see Sidney and Shelby off to school. I took Willie to day care on my way to work at the Capitol.

1961–1966: A NEW LOVE AND POLITICS

The next legislative session was to convene in January of 1961, and I needed a job. I called Bob Eckhardt, a Houston legislator I knew from the 1959 session, whom I respected for his principled voting record in the House, and asked him for a job for the session. He hired me. After hanging up, I had second thoughts: Bob Eckhardt's Houston constituency would mean a heavy workload for me. (Houston legislators had to run from the whole Houston area instead of districts as they do now.) I wanted to be home in time to meet my children after school. I remembered my friend Representative Bob Mullen of Alice, Texas, whose district had more cows than people in it. My workload for him would be light enough to permit me to meet my children after school. He hired me too. I informed Bob Eckhardt that I couldn't work for him, after all. Eckhardt was polite but clearly irritated at the inconvenience of having to find another secretary. And, just my luck, Mullen's desk was right next to Eckhardt's. I tried to make amends by making sure Eckhardt got coffee in the mornings.

Eckhardt wasn't an overt flirt as were so many other members. He was interested in his legislative work, trying to pass good legislation. But he obviously had a woman from Dallas in love with him. He casually left her letters open on top of his desk in full view. I discreetly put them out of sight inside his desk.

It wasn't long before he asked me to lunch. Our mutual interest in politics made for lively conversation. He was recently divorced; I knew his former wife through Jean and Ronnie Dugger. Over many lunches I learned about his family history. His forebears had arrived on the Texas coast around 1840 from the Alsace-Lorraine region of Germany. He was christened Robert Christian Eckhardt, the first of three sons, delivered by their father, Dr. Joe C. A. Eckhardt, at home in Austin on July 17, 1913. His brothers Joe and Norman were born at four-year intervals after Bob. A story oft-repeated has it that Dr. Eckhardt forgot to bring the appropriate string to tie off the umbilical cord, so he used a bacon rind. Stories about his life were of a time when there was a maid in the kitchen, a maid to clean, and a young black man to help care for the several horses. Horseback riding was the primary recreation for the boys who could ride on land stretching west from their house at 23rd and Rio Grande down to Shoal Creek. West beyond the creek and up a high hill lived the black people who worked for families in the Eckhardt neighborhood. Known as Clarksville, the area is prized real estate today. Bob had horses all his life but looked after them marginally. He had artistic and drafting ability and covered the sidewalk around his house with drawings. He erased what he had drawn by rubbing the sidewalk with the seat of the corduroy pants he was wearing before his father, who had a nasty authoritarian temper, got home. For punishment, Bob was locked in a broom closet. When Bob talked about his life growing up, it sounded idyllic except for his father's controlling personality and the conflict between his parents. Bob said he and his brothers thought their parents were on the verge of divorce all the time because the relationship was so volatile. Dr. Eckhardt would accuse Norma of sleeping with the man painting the house or any other man working around the place. He was a model of penury when it came to buying clothing for Norma who was very pretty, social, and loved beautiful clothes. Although the family lived comfortably, she depended on her sisters' hand-medowns for clothing. But Bob had sweet memories of falling asleep in his father's lap in the evenings when they sat on the porch where it was cooler, and he told stories about his father's growing up on the ranch at Yorktown, Texas. Bob was obviously the favorite son and his father wanted him to be a medical doctor. So Bob majored in premed at the University of Texas. But he went to law school instead of medical school. While an undergrad at UT he ran against Jake Pickle for student body president. Jake won. But Bob was the editor of the *Ranger*, the UT magazine, where he could express his art and sense of humor in his cartoons. Jake and Bob both wound up in the U.S. Congress and served together as long as Bob was in Congress. He was part of a set of young people in Austin during the thirties and forties that could've been a forerunner of the crowd in *The Gay Place*. Arty, politically aware, avid readers, the young sophisticates of the era partied as the crowd in *The Gay Place* did in the fifties. He was a very handsome young man who was popular in school and known for his artistic ability. His art, if not his primary interest, was at least a close second. He was tall and had abundant black hair and a southern drawl with a not-unpleasant German twist which resulted in dropped r's at the end of words.

Austin was an idyllic town in those days. It had enough prosperity for the population from the state government and the University of Texas and local commerce. Then, as now, the university and Austin are the center of culture where aspiring, small-town young people from all over the state congregate. Since Bob's family lived close to UT, young relatives would live with the Eckhardts and attend the university. It was a way Dr. Eckhardt could help young relatives from other parts of the state attend college.

Life in Austin included swimming at Barton Springs, where the three Eckhardt brothers met their parents in the summer at 5:00 each afternoon to swim and cool off before dinner. Bob and John Henry Faulk, a judge's son, grew up together. John Henry lived in a big house in South Austin called "Green Pastures." John Henry became famous as a raconteur on radio and television. Bob's other friends included Charles Black, a lawyer's son, who became a constitutional law professor at Yale University and with whom Bob collaborated on a book, *Tides of Power: Conversations on the American Constitution*.

Alcohol figured large in the lives of Bob and his set of friends (as it did with the crowd in *The Gay Place*). Bob repeated stories about his father going out at night to look for him when he didn't come home and finding his son passed out in someone's yard. He didn't leave home until he was twenty-seven, when he married Orissa Stevenson of Houston and joined the U.S. Air Force.

There were politicians on both sides of Bob's family. His grandmother, a Kleberg, married an Eckhardt; the Klebergs and the Eckhardts intermarried twice. The original Bob Kleberg developed the King Ranch after marrying Alice King, the only daughter of Captain Richard King, the founder. Bob's uncle on his mother's side, Harry Wurzbach, had been a U.S. congressman from San Antonio. On the Kleberg side, Bob's Uncle Rudolph had also been a U.S. congressman. Lyndon Johnson's first job in Washington had been as secretary to Congressman Dick Kleberg, a distant cousin of Bob's. Bob always said that the Kleberg side of the family got rich, while the Eckhardt side became doctors and lawyers. Bob and I visited the ranch at Yorktown, which belonged at that time to Dr. Kleberg Eckhardt of Corpus Christi. The house had been kept in its original state by the family. The tack room had saddles with the Running W brand, along with the EK heart brand, a sign that there had been shared ranch hands between the two ranches.

Norma Eckhardt, the former Norma Wurzbach of San Antonio, met the young Dr. Joe Eckhardt in the town of La Grange while at a house party, when she saw him riding a horse down the main street on his way from Galveston Medical School to the Yorktown ranch where he lived. Norma and Joe married and they moved to Austin, where he set up a medical practice. They moved into a big new house at 2300 Rio Grande, that had been bought by Joe's mother. Dr. Eckhardt always had to lie down with his mother before she went to sleep, Norma told me with a note of resentment. Norma was enterprising. She inherited a little money from her family and had two barns behind their house converted into five apartments. After Dr. Eckhardt died, she closed off the staircase in her house and rented the upstairs bedrooms to students. She was able to support herself this way and managed to go to Europe every year with her lady friends. She also had good political instincts. Once when Vice President Johnson was addressing the Texas House of Representatives, she grabbed Bob's hand and made him lead her to the front of the room to shake his hand.

Bob and I began to meet our mutual friends in Austin during the week when the House was in session. He liked to drink and tell stories; he was semi-famous in Texas. Bob introduced me to Ginny and Elmo Hageman, bibliophiles whose house was filled with book stacks and who lived on a hill at Neches and 7th. Ginny was beautiful and Elmo owned the Ritz Theater and didn't have to work very much. So they could stay up all night reading and sleep during the day. Elmo wore his hair long and tied back, a precursor to the Austin hippies. He was a Shakespeare aficionado. When Bob and I visited them when they were awake at night, we had to ring a bell by a gate in a wall in front of the house. Their informed wit and conversation was worth staying up late. Russell Lee, the wonderful photographer known for his Depression-era photos, and Jean, his wife, were already friends of mine and Bob's. Russell photographed Bob for his last campaign for the Texas House of Representatives and for his race for U.S. Congress in 1966. We began to take back-road tours together; we would map out where we were headed, pack a picnic, and spend all day Sunday on the back roads, stopping at inviting places. It seemed to me that it had been a long time since he had had much fun.

THE POWER OF FANTASY

Bob expressed interest in running for Congress several times during our courtship in 1961. I encouraged him, because I knew he had the potential to be a congressman and I thought his chances for election were good. He had a long record as an outstanding labor lawyer and had won difficult cases against Ma Bell for the Communications Workers of America; he had been at the forefront of civil liberties battles in Texas since the forties. Labor and business lobbyists respected his abilities and gave positive assessments about his prospects for higher office, even though some thought he was too liberal.

And I was in love, which I now believe is a form of insanity. Women will perform the most stupid—and sometimes amazing—feats when in love. The old admonition about not sleeping with a man until marriage serves a purpose—I think it becomes impossible to really "see" a man objectively if you're sleeping with him, because it's enjoyable. Bob and I were attracted to each other, both sexually and intellectually, and this was powerful enough to drive us into marriage. Our sexual relationship probably prevented me from recognizing the characteristics that eventually led me to divorce him.

Bob's objective became my objective. He wanted to go to Congress, and I wanted it for him *and* for me. Certain men wind up in the White House or Congress because of the influence of their wives. After meeting and getting to know congressional wives from all parts of the country, I could tell which ones had pushed their husbands and helped them get where they were. Lady Bird Taylor was from Karnack, Texas. A woman of some wealth, she connected with Lyndon. She knew he was going someplace, and she wanted to go, too. Rosalynn Carter probably wanted to get out of Plains, Georgia, for similar reasons. I wanted to go back to D.C. without having to work as a secretary or be separated from my children. I had some idea of how much work being a congressional wife would be after watching Lady Bird work so hard for Lyndon.

I liked being with an older man. Bob called me "Baby" and wrote wonderful love letters. My experience with Billy Lee had convinced me men my own age were irresponsible, and, working under the assumption that men become more responsible with age, I wanted an older, mature man. This included the idea that my children would have a dependable father figure in their lives. The reality of my situation, though, was that I owned my own home, my children were enrolled in the best schools in Austin, and I could have worked at the Capitol or for a state agency until I retired.

But I knew Bob was ready for the U.S. Congress because I had spent two and a half years observing the U.S. Senate and House when I worked for Lyndon. My vision was so compelling and my gut instinct so certain, I decided I would marry this mature, attractive, talented man, create a wonderful home life, help him achieve a congressional seat, and return to Washington as a congressional wife. Consciously, I was marrying Bob because I loved him and wanted to help him in his political career. Subconsciously, I think I was the one who really wanted to go to Congress.

Bob and I married in March of 1962, and during the next four years our time was divided between Houston and Austin. During legislative sessions, we lived in Austin. In between sessions, we lived in a small shack on fifteen acres of land that he owned in the section of Harris County that was most likely to elect him. The heavily wooded land was beautiful, but living there was difficult at times, especially at first. Initially there was no electricity or water well; it was incredibly hot and sticky in the summer. I cooked on a hot plate or an open fire. Sidney, Shelby, and Willie had mixed feelings about our situation—they liked the country setting, but they missed Austin. They were used to Austin's good schools, and attending the rural school in nearby Spring, Texas, which entailed catching a bus at the end of the dirt road, was quite a change. Switching schools every other year when the Texas legislature was in session was also a challenge.

The life of a legislator, whether on a state or a national level, requires an enormous amount of socializing. Invitations flowed from every special interest group imaginable: the beer lobby, the labor lobby, the oil lobby, the highway lobby, you name it. Lobbyists are usually gregarious types—most often ex-legislators who host parties in order to schmooze in a congenial and relaxed (i.e., drunken) atmosphere, when members are more at ease. Some legislators choose to avoid these soirees altogether, as the social grind gets tiresome after a year or two. But if you're going after higher office, the necessary campaign funding can only be built by a network of lobbyists who can acquire the funding. You have to be on the scene socially, so Bob and I were on the go to political meetings and parties much of the time, even attending several functions in different parts of Harris County in one evening. I changed clothes in filling station restrooms when necessary. While the long-term goal was to get Bob into the Congress, the immediate concerns were getting the children off to school, getting Bob off to work, hauling groceries, cooking, chauffeuring children to acting or music lessons, coordinating with Bob's secretary about various invitations, and inviting friends and colleagues to our house for dinner.

Living in such primitive circumstances fueled our desire to build a larger house, but this was difficult on an isolated, rural piece of virgin property. Fortunately, Bob had a friend from his Air Force days, a capable contractor, who brought his assistant and set up headquarters in the only motel on the interstate. Our big new house was built in three months—record time—thanks to the efforts of the contractor and to me pushing for speed. We moved in on November 3, 1963, at the end of Bamwood Drive, on Cypress Creek in Harris County.

Needless to say, we were all thrilled to have a real home that accommodated our needs. Our lives seemed to be falling into place. Then, as if on schedule, I got pregnant again. Bob had two daughters from his first marriage, Orissa (fifteen) and Rosalind (fourteen), when we married. His ex-wife had been in and out of a private mental hospital and was undergoing shock treatment for manic depression. I was shocked by all of this, even more so when I learned that their divorce had been precipitated by an affair Bob had been having for years with one of his ex's friends (I remembered the love letters I had discreetly hidden in his desk a couple of years earlier that were obviously from the same woman).

Bob's younger daughter Rosalind had a difficult time adjusting to our marriage. She asked him to exclude me when she and Bob were together. His older daughter escaped the situation by spending time with her friends and staying in Europe. My children didn't exhibit any specific problems at the time, but the effects of the marriage and all the change would manifest themselves later, as they became teenagers and young adults.

If Bob and I had been mature, thinking adults, we never would have married so quickly, or perhaps not at all. Sometime during my pregnancy in 1964, I felt we had to deal with our growing problems: his daughters' difficulties regarding his new marriage, my feelings of unhappiness at being excluded at his daughter's request, and a host of other issues. Bob didn't want to confront or even talk about the problem. I went to a family therapist to vent, and he advised me that my husband would have to join in the therapy in order to resolve the situation. But I had married a man who had been raised by an authoritarian father whose disciplinary efforts bordered on abuse, and he was resistant to therapy even if it was in the best interest of his family.

Bill had stopped sending child support payments after Bob and I married. And he was suffering from his much-discussed writer's block—he couldn't seem to get going on another book or even fulfill a short writing assignment. On September 13, 1963, at a hearing in Austin, I apprised the court that Bill wasn't paying child support and that I had heard film rights for *The Gay Place* had been sold to Paul Newman and Martin Ritt for $25,000. I wanted some action to be taken by the court.

But Bill didn't show. I knew his whereabouts, generally. He had worked for Stuart Long's news service for a bit, in early 1963, and had lived for a short time with Larry McMurtry on Windsor Road in Austin. Then he moved into an apartment on Brazos, near the Capitol. Several beautiful young women lived upstairs, including Dorothy Browne, with whom Bill became an item. It took some time before the judicial system ground out a subpoena, which was delivered to Bill at the garage apartment where he lived behind another of Larry McMurtry's houses, this one in the Rice University neighborhood of Houston. The subpoena gave Bill impetus to take Ken Kesey up on his invitation to visit him in California, so he fled west to El Paso and on to California, as so many other men have done to escape responsibility for debts, wives, and the law. I knew that Bill would spend the money immediately if he got his hands on it, so I had to act quickly to acquire the interest the children and I had coming. I contacted Gene Palmer, my lawyer, who coordinated the garnishment of our share. A sheriff in New York picked up the check from the office of Bill's agent, Elizabeth McKee.

TRAGEDY AND THE AFTERMATH

On the night of November 21, 1963, Bob and I attended a dinner in Houston honoring Congressman Albert Thomas. President Kennedy and Jackie were there, and both made brief speeches. Jackie delivered hers in Spanish, which pleased the Mexican-American attendees immeasurably. As we left the convention center, a man handed us a leaflet reminding us that not everyone in Texas was happy to have the president visiting our state.

Kennedy was killed in Dallas the next day. Bob, the children, and I were in shock—we stayed glued to our black-and-white TV for days. I first heard the news in my car, as I was driving the twenty-five miles from Houston to our house, and my initial reaction was to think that some maniac John Bircher had killed the president. When I heard the news that he had been murdered by a "Communist," I immediately came to the conclusion that it had been a setup.

Bob and I watched LBJ take the oath of office while Lady Bird and Jackie stood by. Our friend, Jack Valenti, also a Houstonian, was whisked off to Washington—he had married Mary Margaret Wiley and settled in Houston, but Lyndon needed them with him, so they pulled up their roots and moved to D.C., where they were involved with the new administration. I would miss Jack Kennedy, who had been so inspiring, but I had confidence in Lyndon's presidential abilities.

Just after the assassination, Bill was visiting his parents in Dallas. He was at the Dallas Police Headquarters when Jack Ruby shot

Lee Harvey Oswald. He immediately received several writing offers, including an assignment to write a story on Lady Bird for *Ladies' Home Journal,* plus an $11,000 advance with the promise of $1,000 per chapter from Random House to write a biography of LBJ.

Bill and Dorothy Browne were married in Houston in December of 1963. Bill received an advance from New American Library: $10,000 plus $1,000 for every chapter of a novel of his choosing. It was never fulfilled. (Later, in 1965, Bill received another contract from New American Library, for a potential $50,000 for two novels of his choice. These remained unfulfilled as well.) Bill and Dorothy went to Washington and rented Marie and Glen Wilson's basement apartment so Bill could try to fulfill his various writing assignments, but his attempts to interview Lady Bird were stonewalled by the White House. Finally, he was informed by George Reedy that he was persona non grata at the White House. Bill theorized that Lady Bird was the reason for the snub: he thought that she had read *The Gay Place* (whose character "Sweet Mama" does not depict her in the most endearing light) and he believed that she had given Lyndon a bad report about it. "Lyndon doesn't read anything but memos," Bill said, adding, "and Lady Bird didn't understand it." But, in light of much else that was written about Johnson during the sixties, *The Gay Place* was a literary tribute.

After the rebuff from the White House, Bill and Dorothy moved to Mexico and lived for a time in Manzanillo, Acapulco, and Mexico City. The proceeds from the sale of the film rights to *The Gay Place* relaxed our financial situation a bit. I bought a washing machine, a dryer, and a new American Rambler four-door sedan. By September of 1964, I was about ready to pop, and on September 18 Sarah Eckhardt was born.

Having four children, a husband, and several animals was a heavy load, but I was thirty-three (Sidney was twelve, Shelby, ten, and Willie, seven) and I was energetic and stimulated by the times. After the shock and sadness of the Kennedy assassination, President Johnson defeated Senator Barry Goldwater in 1964 and, having earned the presidency in his own right, was proceeding confidently. His power increased enormously in Texas. He was getting legislation passed that might have been impossible under President Kennedy.

Bob and I were proceeding on course, politically. The tensions caused by our family problems didn't deter us from our mutual goal: getting him elected to Congress. He had passed a good piece of legislation in the Texas House called the Open Beaches Bill, which prevented private interests from buying up beachfront property and excluding access to the public. He had a wide group of supporters among Houston liberals, and although conservatives didn't like his politics, they respected him personally. Bob was politically wily. He knew how to play to the media and get the most exposure out of an issue. He had good ideas but he sometimes lacked follow-through, relying on others to implement his actions.

We were concerned about Bob's mother living alone in her big Victorian house in Austin, so we moved into it for the special session of the legislature in 1965. Mrs. Eckhardt needed help with everyday living. Bob and his brothers arranged for her to move to a high-rise development for seniors in Houston where she had her own apartment and plenty of friends with whom to play cards, her favorite activity. The children and I loved living in Mrs. Eckhardt's house and had fun discovering old sheet music, old clothes—old everything. Cleaning the house was a major project. The family had lived there for the past fifty years and Mrs. Eckhardt had saved everything. Bob's law practice, his legislative duties, and the difficulties with his younger daughter and her mother kept him constantly traveling back and forth from Austin to Houston. He and I were at a stalemate as far as Rosalind was concerned. She remained upset at our marriage; we continued to spend weekends apart, so that he could spend time with her. I decided to stay on in the Eckhardt's Austin house after the session was over rather than return to our home in Houston—if he persisted in keeping us separate, I would rather be separate in Austin than in Houston. Rosalind had had back surgery that necessitated bed rest for several months and Bob wanted his daughter to convalesce at our place in Houston. During the summer of 1965 while Rosalind recuperated, Bob's ex-wife committed suicide. Bob certainly needed my emotional support and I attended the funeral in Houston. I returned to Austin feeling depressed, but the reality of having to care for four children didn't leave time for feelings.

Sometime that summer during our stay in Mrs. Eckhardt's house, Bill paid a visit to offer to pay Sidney's tuition to attend St. Stephen's Episcopal School in the hills near Austin. It is a school admired and cherished by ex-students. Of course, Sidney wanted to attend as a boarding student. She had a happy and productive year and her grades made her eligible for a scholarship for the following school year. But at the end of the school year I received a phone call: Bill had never paid the tuition and Sidney couldn't have the scholarship unless the previous year's fees were paid.

There is no fury like that of a mother whose child has been wronged or hurt. To make matters worse, Bob was supporting the children and me, and I felt that it was doubly unfair of Bill to renege on paying court-imposed child support. The children and I had returned to Houston in time for their school year, but I knew that Bill and Dorothy were back in Austin—and that he had rented one of the old West Avenue mansions, which in itself was typical Bill, living beyond his means. I jumped in my car, my blood boiling, and drove directly to his house, ready to do bodily harm. My mission as I drove to Austin was to beat him to a pulp, and I entered the house like a madwoman yelling how he had betrayed Sidney. Bill, along with the hangers-on at his house, ran like cockroaches. Sidney and Shelby and Willie enrolled in the Spring, Texas, schools in 1966, and our lives were again absorbed in politics. I was still young and confident; I still thought I was in love. Otherwise, this period of conflict and sadness would have overwhelmed me.

THE RUN FOR CONGRESS

It was the last day in 1965 for filing for the congressional seat occupied by Albert Thomas. Hartsell Gray, our friend, and I drove Bob to the Harris County courthouse and issued a statement saying that

Bob was filing as an alternative candidate because Congressman Thomas was sick with advanced prostate cancer. Ten days after Bob filed, Congressman Thomas died. Then came the inevitable call from Congressman Jack Brooks, telling Bob that Thomas's wife wanted to fulfill her husband's term. Bob deferred making a decision and after a few days of intense media speculation, announced that he would step aside for the lady "at this time" but would remain a candidate in the next election. This gave us more time to organize.

At the same time, in the Memorial area, the district west of the 8th, young George H. W. Bush was also running for Congress. I invited George and Barbara to a picnic on Cypress Creek. The party on the large, white-sand creek bed was a great setting in which to get to know each other. There was a fire, steaks, wine, and an interesting mix of journalists, labor types, and politicos. George has a fun, childlike quality, and I loved his silly streak. And Barbara's lack of pretension has charmed many.

Bob and George had much to talk about, comparing campaigns. Both of them were articulate, attractive, and intelligent. They spoke about problems with the "nuts" in their parties: George's extreme right-wingers and Bob's extreme left-wingers. George told a story of being surrounded by some UN haters at a political meeting and having to physically fend them off. Later, Bob told him that he would help him out by publicly attacking him as an "extreme right-winger" the next time George was being hassled; George said he would do the same for Bob.

Bob and George had lively debates, including one memorable one at Texas A&M University that kept everyone not only awake but also amused. We later termed these debates "The George and Bob Show." The two politicians seemed to cue each other's best lines, and they both had a good sense of humor, which was very much appreciated by the audience. They were naturals, which boded well for both of them.

After an intense and exhausting year of campaigning, going to meetings, and working with volunteers, Bob was elected to Congress in 1966. It was a great feeling to accomplish our long-term goal—I had been moving so fast that 1966 was a blur. The night of the election, Bob and I drove across Harris County to George and Barbara's campaign headquarters to congratulate them. They never forgot it, and the four of us saw each other a great deal during the ensuing years in D.C.

I was a little anxious about LBJ's response to Bob's election, for Bob would be the most liberal member of the Texas delegation. And I didn't know how Johnson would react to me, either; I hadn't seen him for several years. I was relieved to hear through the grapevine that when Harry McPherson told the president that Bob had been elected, Lyndon said, "He's a *bred* congressman." The comment was pure Lyndon and very reassuring.

Before Congress convened in January of 1967, we house-hunted in Washington and were lucky enough to find a charming place in Georgetown, just across the street from the house that the Kennedys lived in when Jack was in the Senate. The house, at 3312 N Street NW, was perfect for our needs—a four-story town house with plenty of bedrooms, two large living rooms, a kitchen, a dining room, and a small sitting room in the basement. Rent was reasonable at $400 a month. And it was in the city.

After three days in the car with all the children, we arrived in D.C. just in time for a snowstorm. We didn't care—we were in D.C. and it was snowing! Elated about living in Georgetown after so many years in the country, we walked down the middle of N Street, sidewalks piled high with snow, to Martin's Tavern, President Harry Truman's old hangout, where we sat together and ate a good meal as we watched the snow.

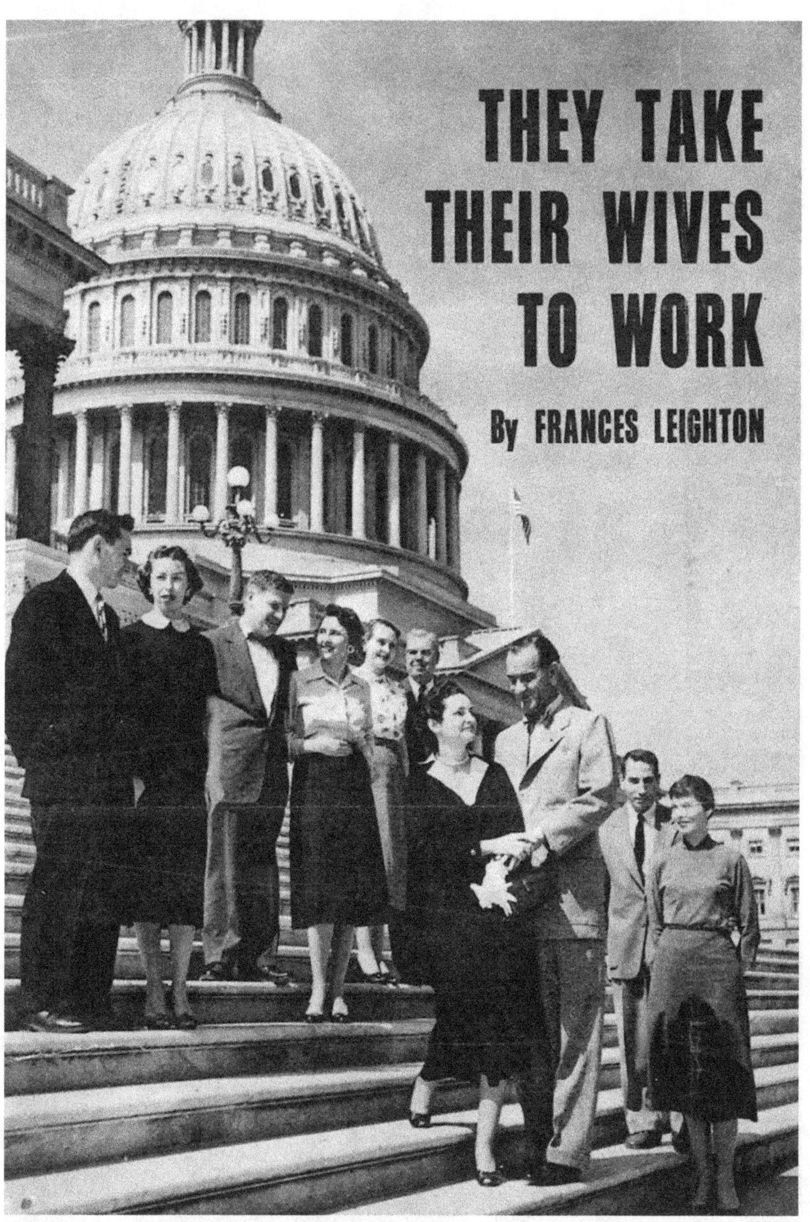

Bill and I on the steps of the Capitol, with Lyndon Johnson, Lady Bird Johnson, John and Ann Leonarz, Glen and Marie Wilson, and Glynn and Mildred Stegall, August 26, 1956.

Nadine Ellen Thompson, my mother, circa 1925.

Leslie Wells, my biological father, at the organ
in Oklahoma City, circa mid-1920s.

Noah Lee Cannon, "Daddy Noah," leaving to go to work, circa late 1940s.

Rio Grande Valley towns sponsor a "Citrus Fiesta" to promote tourism. I was chosen as Duchess of Palms to represent McAllen, the City of Palms. Later, Bill Brammer called me "Duchess of Psalms."

Billy Lee Brammer, circa 1948–1949. Bill was a great diver and baseball player.

During a walk on the North Texas State campus,
Bill asked if he could take this picture, circa 1950.

Nadine Cannon, eighteen-year-old sophomore at North Texas State University, 1950.

Collegians Say Vows

Nadine Cannon, daughter of Mr. and Mrs. Noah Cannon, Mc-Allen, and Bill Brammer, son of Mr. and Mrs. H. L. Brammer, Dallas, were married April 22. They will make their home here.

The bride, a sophomore here, attended Edinburg junior college. Brammer, a junior journalism student, attended the University of Texas.

Announcement of my marriage to Bill, April 22, 1950, in the McAllen *Monitor.*

The Austin American
MORNING
The Austin Statesman
EVENING
Sunday American-Statesman
SUNDAY

SEVENTH AT COLORADO · AUSTIN, TEXAS

Thursday

Mond Lisa:

Still getting christmas cards from people I didn't send any to. Send to the following if you have any left. Roy Terrell and Emil Tag at the C-T. ~~Mx~~ Mr. and Mrs. Morris Williams c/o American Statesman (Better put our last names ~~xxxxxxxxxx~~ somewhere on that one). Mebbie Don Carr if we have any cards left, also. Bought Cathy a prazunt today, so no need to get one for her. Spent two bucks on a paint set or something. It's already mailed. Try to get your folks and my folks somethin nice....charge it....and we'll pay when I get down there. Just sent you a letter couple of hours ago, and this will probably get there before that one. Guess that is all. Miss you,

Merry Jesus

Note from Bill while I was in McAllen recovering from pregnancy sickness, Christmas 1951.

Mary Margaret Wiley (later Mrs. Jack Valenti) on the right knee of Harry McPherson, with me on his left knee, at a party at Jean and Ronnie Dugger's house, winter 1954. Taken just before we all went to Washington to work for LBJ.

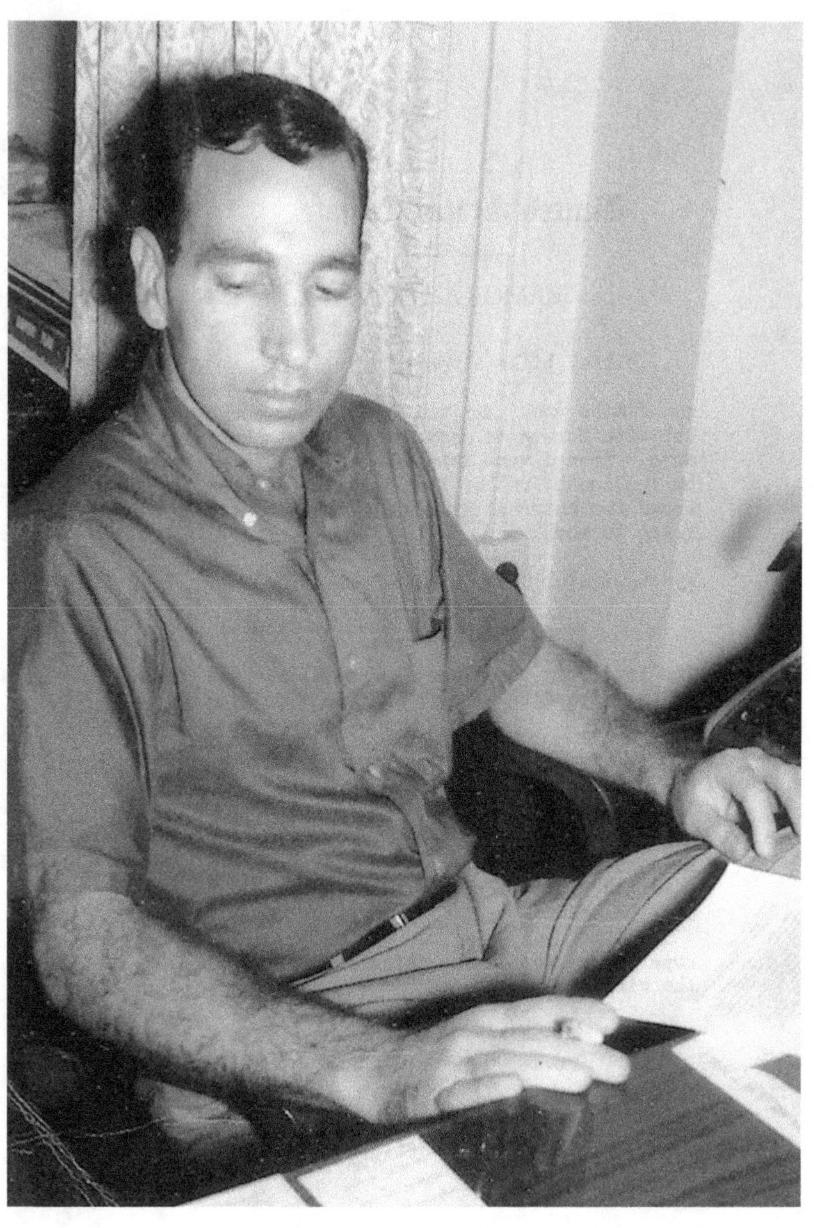

Bill in LBJ's Austin office, 1955. Photo by Pat Mathis.

United States Senate

MEMORANDUM

...bills, bills already

And I miss you. Arrived at 4:30 and caught a cab with Norman to Mary Margaret's to get his auto. Then I went into SOB and went to sleep on the couch, rather than take the trouble to spend two hours at Arlington Towers before going to work.

My check stub says: $40 to Safeway
$110 to Dr. Bailey
$100 cash at Capital Natl

The latter is for plane fare back, license plates, and $10 spending money. What do I do when it runs out?

Wrote to Street today and hope it won't be long before it hits something.

I may be in Texas in middle of April with LBJ. He's having the meeting I suggested at ranch with his county men, and either Booth or I will be around.

Hope you're not disappointed in the house. Love the girls.

And send me the key to 201 on our keychain.

yassuh

Note from Bill, early 1955.

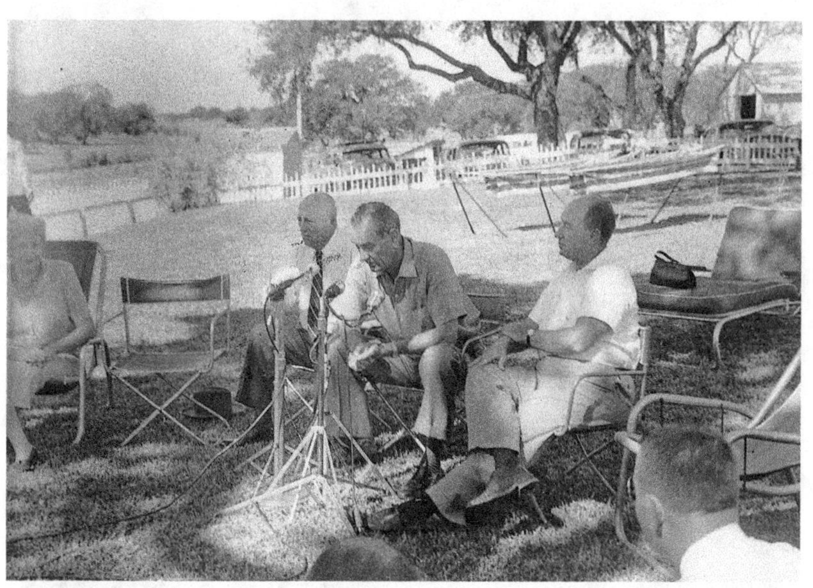

Left to right: Grace Tully, Sam Rayburn, Lyndon Johnson, and Adlai Stevenson at a press conference during Johnson's recuperation from his heart attack at the ranch in Johnson City, summer of 1955. Photo by Bill Brammer.

Bill and Nadine Brammer in the backyard of their home in Austin, 1955.

LYNDON B. JOHNSON
TEXAS

STATE OFFICE:
207 U. S. Courthouse
Austin, Texas

United States Senate
Office of the Democratic Leader
Washington, D. C.
May 9, 1957

Dear Nadine:

I consider that an irrevocable promise and I intend to hold you to it!

You are a mighty sweet girl and you give me a great deal of comfort for which I am very grateful.

I hope you are doing all right and I'll try to send Bill back down there before too long.

Regards.

Sincerely,

Lyndon B. Johnson

Mrs. Bill Brammer
2210 Enfield Road
Austin, Texas

LBJ wrote me this note upon my resignation from his staff in 1957.

Bill looking artsy at MOMA in New York,
May 1958. Photo by Ina Stewart (now Schoenberg).

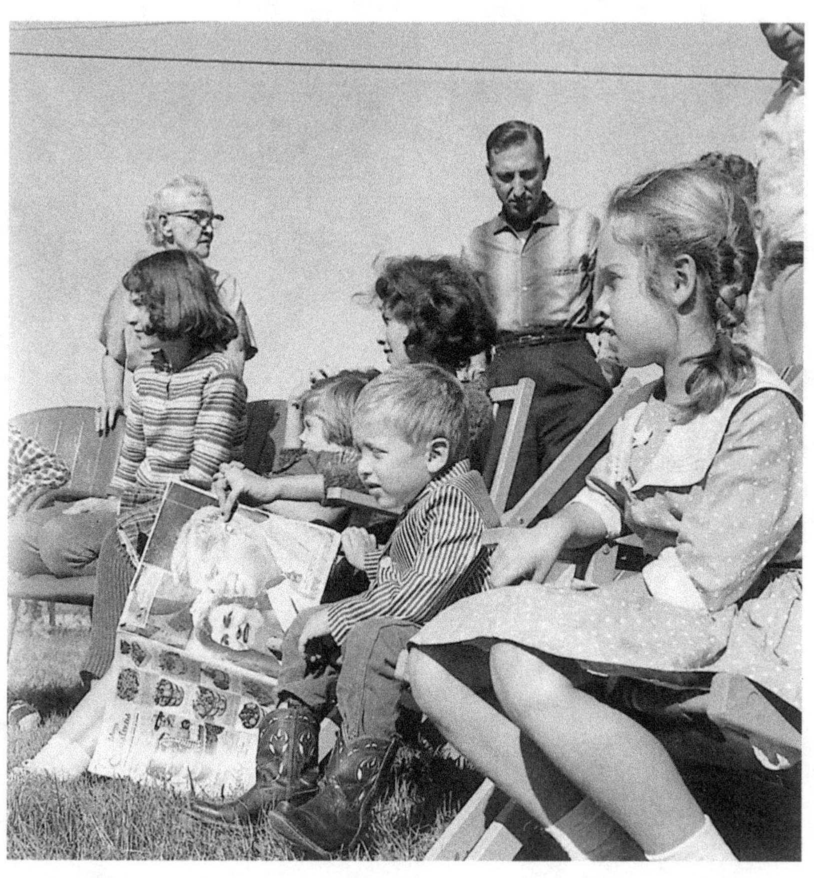

Nadine Brammer, center, surrounded by children, Shelby, Willie, and Sidney. Left to right: Kathy Gunnell, Bill's niece; Kate Brammer, Bill's mother; Jim Brammer, Bill's brother.

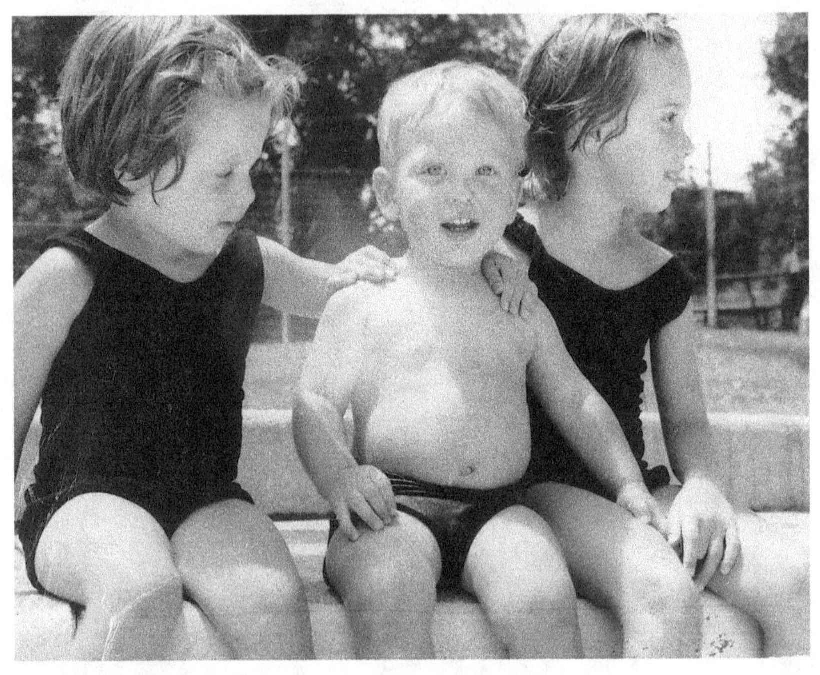

Shelby, Willie, and Sidney Brammer at swimming pool in Austin, circa 1959.

EDITORIAL ROOM

April 59

HOUGHTON MIFFLIN COMPANY

2 PARK STREET BOSTON 7

April 2, 1959

Mr. William Brammer
231 Senate Office Building
Washington, D. C.

Dear Bill:

The finished "twins" and the stories arrived safely and we are still getting readings on them. Then we will have to argue some, then you will hear. This happens to be a season when the office is really loaded and things are moving more slowly than usual. But Brammer has been "active" since his arrival: I promise you he is not gathering dust in the files.

Walter Prescott Webb is one of our greatest prides and I am sending you a copy of AN HONEST PREFACE under separate cover.

You are being redundant when you refer to yourself as "the perfect neurotic author". Just say author and I know all. Don't worry (<u>that</u> advice helps a lot!) and try to let this idea grow to full size, about 200 pages more than usual. You'll hear.

Yours ever,

Mrs. G. D. de Santillana

DC/jw

Mrs. G. D. de Santillana, managing editor of Houghton Mifflin, was an early champion of *The Gay Place.* She helped envision the trilogy format and shepherd the book through its publication.

CABLE ADDRESS
HOUGHTON BOSTON

The Riverside Press
Cambridge 38, Massachusetts

HOUGHTON MIFFLIN COMPANY

2 PARK STREET · BOSTON 7

June 26, 1959

Mr. Bill Brammer
5123 New Senate Office Building
Washington, D. C.

Dear Bill:

I have just finished IF EVER ANY BEAUTY as practically my last official act until my return. It is wonderful reading, it has swing and glitter and pace. The people, even those who are only briefly on stage, are real and round. Governor Fenstemaker is GREAT.

But you have a little more work to do on it. I know what you are trying to say. But as a "reader" I don't know it, I'm confused. And although the technical end--in the Capitol fountain--is fine, and the stream of consciousness a brilliant tour de force. You have got to do some more work on this chapter.

I think you have tried not to be explicit and I think you have got to be quite explicit and specific. I think the reader at present is unsatisfied, in the air. I think you've got to tell him right out 1) that the Democratic nomination in Texas means Neil is elected (this is small and technical) 2) on what terms he faces his public future and his private present.

Think about this some and don't rush it. It means, I think, only work on the last chapter. For everything else, many congratulations. When you get this revision fixed up will you mail it direct to Paul Brooks. Have a good summer. In the fall we must get together. And talk about Arthur Fenstemaker who is rapidly becoming my great American Hero--you've got to really build him in the next!

Congratulations and best wishes,

Yours,

Mrs. G. D. de Santillana

DS/jw

Another perfectly diplomatic and enthusiastic note from de Santillana.

HOUGHTON MIFFLIN COMPANY

NEW YORK 16
432 FOURTH AVE.
CORNER 29TH STREET

April 12, 1960

Mr. William Brammer
Janeway Publishing and Research Corporation, Inc.
Empire State Building
New York, New York

Dear Bill:

Feeling that IF EVER ANY BEAUTY is the most successful book of your trilogy, I am returning its revision with little adverse comment. I feel that dialogue, narrative, sections dealing with characterizations are sharp, sensitive, comic in the right places, and touching. While this novel resolves little--and I don't believe it is your point to force a resolution--, I believe your picture of Texan political life a convincing and sincere one. Neil's domestic problems with Andrea and the children are artistically handled, and one believes that someday--outside the novel, of course--Neil and Andrea will come together again in love: I could not help but sense a certain optimism in their confused affair of marriage. This is a good novel, and it fits very well and dramatically into the center of the trilogy.

In Chapter Thirteen, page 155, four lines from the bottom of the page, I think it would be a good idea to delete the mention of Eisenhower. This reference will date the book. Also, beginning at the bottom of page 155 and continuing through the top of page 156, you have bits of overheard conversation. I rebel at this: the technique has been used to death in other novels.

Also, might you mention at the beginning of this book that the scene is again Texas? In the GAY PLACE the setting <u>is</u> Texas. Nowhere in IF EVER ANY BEAUTY is Texas mentioned.

I wish to commend you on the passage on page 254 beginning <u>"Blotting sand?..."</u> There are many sections just as good as this that illustrate the work of a good writer. I only cite this as an example of one of the facets of your writing that I like very much.

God save Governor Fenstermaker!

Sam

Samuel D. Stewart
New York Editor

SDS/bk

MS returned under separate cover by messenger—

From another editor at Houghton Mifflin, Samuel Stewart.

1119:46

CABLE ADDRESS
HOUGHTON BOSTON

The Riverside Press
Cambridge 38, Massachusetts

HOUGHTON MIFFLIN COMPANY

2 PARK STREET · BOSTON 7

June 3, 1960

Mr. Bill Brammer
Janeway Publishing & Research Corp.
Suite 5901
Empire State Building
New York 1, New York

Dear Bill:

First things first: Paul has read the novel and likes it as much as the rest of us, so you be as happy as I am.

Second: Sam has written me about the name to be used as official author: No one, I repeat no one, up here thinks "Billy Lee" is possible. With all respect to your parents who gave it to you with such evident love (it is a very "loving" name) it has not the strength and authority for a novel which commands respect at the top of its voice.

We are going to call it "by B. L. Brammer" and if we are asked we shall answer "Bill L. Brammer". This is official!

Time swings along! I still haven't got to New York but I am absolutely certainly coming between the 15th and the 30th when I depart, so we will have a small celebration. I will let you know in time.

Feel good, everything's fine!

Yours,

Dorothy de Santillana

Mrs. G. D. de Santillana

JW

DS/jw
Dictated but not read

From the ever-upbeat de Santillana, breaking the news that "Billy Lee" as a pen name was not "possible."

Bob Eckhardt, campaign photo, early 1960s. Photo by Russell Lee.

THE Statler Hilton ST. LOUIS
COMPLETELY AIR CONDITIONED
Washington Ave. • Ninth & St. Charles Sts. • St. Louis 1, Mo.

Dear Nadine,

I wonder if it is because I am used to the particular brand of ugliness of southern women that I don't notice it anymore and conclude that the midwest is populated by females that could hardly raise a man to the effort of propogating his species. Here — and I remember in Toledo — women have a kind of midle European stolidity. Come to think of it, men do too — they were born of women — but they are not so noticeable because they are not set off in a frame of furs and feathers. But they look like this:

(Come to think of it, they are even

HILTON HOTELS LOCATED IN PRINCIPAL CITIES AROUND THE WORLD

Bob was a wonderful cartoonist and often illustrated his letters with sketches. In 1996, an exhibit of his drawings was put up at the Center for American History at the University of Texas.

The Austin Statesman

The Oldest Afternoon Newspaper In Texas

Vol. 92—No. 250 | Austin, Texas, Thursday, May 16, 1963 | 2 Parts—52 Pages 10 Cents

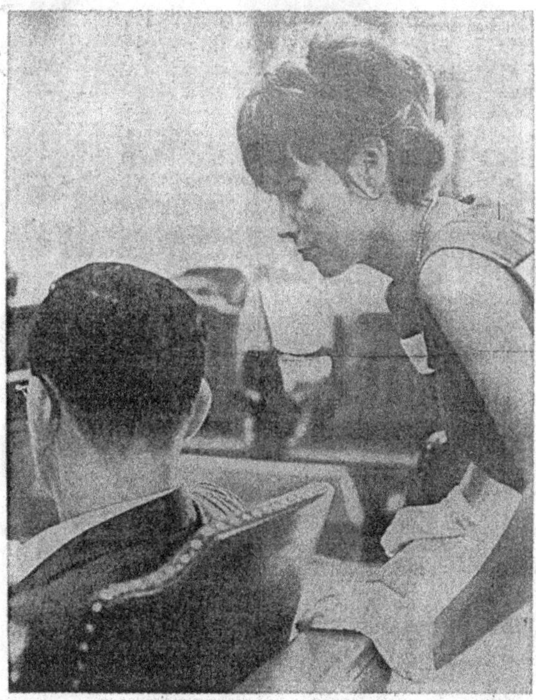

American-Statesman/UPI

MRS. ROBERT ECKHARDT'S BILL OF DISCOVERY GRANTED IN COURT

She wants to know how much ex-husband's "Gay Place" has made

Brammer's Ex-Wife

Court Backs Her

By AL WILLIAMS

The former wife of award-winning novelist Bill Brammer has the right to know how much money he has received from the sale of "The Gay Place", 126th District Court Judge Jack Roberts ruled Thursday.

Mrs. Robert Eckhardt, whose divorce judgment from Brammer on June 27, 1961, awarded her one-half interest in the book, said she has received no concrete information — and no money — on royalties or from the rumored sale of movie rights to the book.

She said she had heard from friends, and her own children, that movie rights had been sold to "The Gay Place", but she said, "I have no proof whatsoever."

Under questioning by her attorney, Gene Palmer, she said her ex-husband had told her he received $2,000 in advance on a movie option contract. "He promised me half, but I didn't see half,' she said.

"I want to find out exactly how much has been paid or will be paid," she stated, saying she would use all of the proceeds for the three children which resulted from her marriage to Brammer.

She denied that she first heard of the movie rights of the book from Brammer in answer to the question from Brammer's attorney

(See AUTHOR, Page A5)

AUTHOR

(Continued from Page One)

Brooks Holman, if it wasn't true that Brammer telephoned her with the information.

"He certainly did not telephone me," she exclaimed. She said she thought she heard it first from her children.

"You do not recollect a call from your ex-husband that he thought you would be interested in the good news and that he was excited and wanted you to know?"

"I have questioned and questioned and questioned and have not heard anything definite," said Mrs. Eckhardt. "That's why my attorney filed a bill of inquiry to find out what was going on. I had knowledge of a contract but no details," she said.

"I want every little tiny bit of information I can get to let me know when my children will get what is coming to them. I want my children to have all the benefit from the contract," she said.

On Holman's question, she said she would "be just overjoyed if Brammer would sign an instrument letting the movie company know that half of the money should go to me and the children before it goes to his creditors."

She said if she knew the details of the movie contract she wouldn't be in court. "I want the money for my three little children, not for myself," she said.

In ruling that "relief sought by the plaintiff is granted", Judge Roberts told the attorneys that certified copies of the divorce should be sent to the "collective agents" or whoever is handling payments on the book to put them on notice that Mrs. Eckhardt is entitled to half interest in all payments.

Under terms of the contract with Dover Productions, which Holman had in court, Brammer was to receive $2,000 in advance for the movie option on the book. He is scheduled to receive $20,000 if the movie company — headed by Paul Newman — exercises the option and another $5,000 when the film is actually shot.

The book by Brammer won a Houghton Mifflin award and critical acclaim.

In court in Austin, trying to drum up child support after I had heard that *The Gay Place* would be made into a movie. The movie's production was nixed by a call from the White House after LBJ became president.

Bob and I just after moving into the house we built in Harris County, November 1963. Photo by Johnny Huber.

Posing on the steps of the Capitol before a lunch date. Left to right: Bob Eckhardt, Bob Pierpoint (ABC newsman), Barbara Bush, myself, Jessica Catto, George H. W. Bush, and Bill Hobby, 1967.

President Johnson, myself, and Bob at the Bayou Club in Houston for an event honoring John Connally, 1969.

Bob and I on Air Force One, on our way to
an event in Austin honoring President Johnson.

HOUSE OF REPRESENTATIVES
WASHINGTON, D. C.

GEORGE BUSH
TEXAS-7TH DISTRICT

November 16, 1970

Dear Nadine:

You're a thoughtful girl, indeed.

Part of the problem is I thought we were going to win, and thus defeat was tougher to accept. But, we've had a week roughing it in the Bahamas, and somehow life doesn't seem all that desperate now. I don't know whether we're going to stay here or not, but, in any event, it's kind of fun to contemplate the future. Let's contemplate it a little more some evening.

We saw Bob in Houston. I accused him of having a haircut, but he denied it with some vehemence. Perhaps this is because he was with one of his constituents. In any event, he looked great and his words were comforting and reassuring. The Eckhardts somehow have always had a special place in our hearts, and I'm not just talking about politics. But, since Bob was the only one to kind of stand up against the Connally machine, the place has become even more special.

Warm regards,

Note I received from George H. W. Bush, in response to a condolence letter I had written after he lost the 1970 senatorial race to Lloyd Bentsen.

Left to right: Bob Eckhardt, Bill Hobby, Frank Sinatra, Nadine Eckhardt, and Mack Hofheinz backstage at Hofheinz Pavilion, before Sinatra concert, November 1974.

Bob Eckhardt and Bill Hobby presenting Frank Sinatra with a Texas hat before his performance at Hofheinz Pavilion in Houston, November 1974.

Left to right: Susan Streit (who later married Jerry Jeff Walker), Nadine Eckhardt, Bob Eckhardt, and Mack Hofheinz, backstage at Hofheinz Pavilion in Houston, November 1974.

Bill, circa late 1970s.

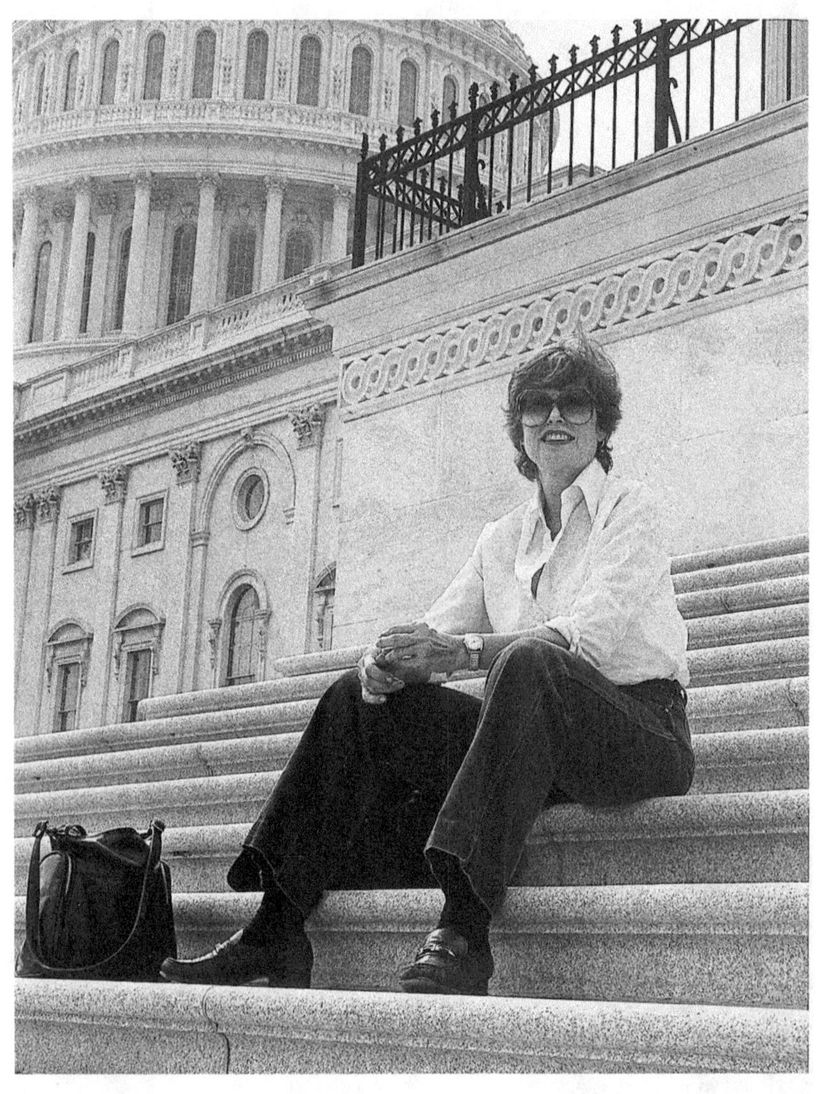

On the steps of the Capitol, 1983. Photo by Lou Linden.

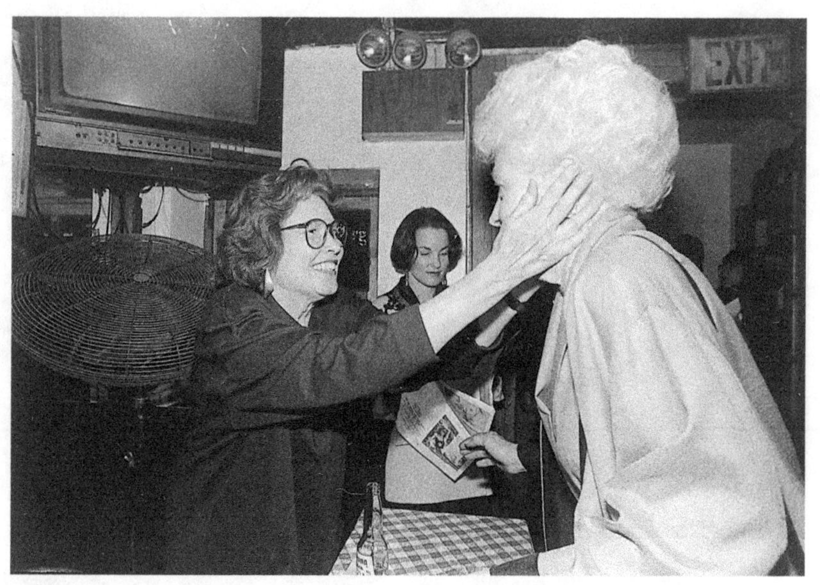

At a fund-raiser for Ann Richards, New York City, 1990. Photo by Ave Bonar.

Shelby, Sarah, Willie, myself, and Sidney, in 2002. Photo by Alan Pogue.

NADINE ECKHARDT

2110 La Casa	Austin, Texas 78704	(512) 442-9672

PERSONAL & CONFIDENTIAL

February 28, 2003

Dear George,

You were sweet and thoughtful to write to Bob Eckhardt's daughters after his death. We all appreciate it.

When we sort of caught up with each other's doings, you said you were trying to keep out of your son's business. I think we can generally agree that it's wise to stay out of our children's business. However, when we see one of them doing something self-defeating or harming someone else, all we can do is let them know how we feel and think about it. Whether or not they take our advice is up to them. All we can do is register our advice and, hopefully, our wisdom. And hope they know we love them enough to risk wounding their ego a bit.

As one parent to another and an admirer of your and Barbara's long experience in politics and government, I urge you to get <u>into</u> your son's business. Our nation needs your wisdom, George.

If you need mine, call me.

Best of everything to you and Barbara,

Nadine

Letter of February 20, 2003, to President George H. W. Bush urging him to exert his wisdom in his son's decision to go to war in Iraq.

GEORGE BUSH

March 10, 2003

Dear Nadine,

Thanks for your letter.

I am very happy to be on the sidelines. I do talk regularly to the President, but it is not to give advice. I am just there as his dad. He has my full confidence.

The President is facing an enormous number of extraordinarily difficult problems, and he is holding up pretty darn well. Have faith!

Warm regards,

Mrs. Nadine Eckhardt
2110 La Casa
Austin, TX 78704

Letter of March 10, 2003, from President George H. W. Bush saying he had full confidence in his son. Eighteen days later, we went to war in Iraq.

1967–1969: LIFE AS A CONGRESSIONAL WIFE

Ten years after leaving the employ of Senate Majority Leader Lyndon Johnson, I was back in Washington as a congressional wife, living in Georgetown. LBJ had been president for three years. This was long-delayed and hard-won gratification, for I believed in my heart that my husband would never have been elected to the House of Representatives without my support. I thought that I would be an integral part of his operation, an extension of his staff. We were a team and there would be no limits to what we could accomplish for the good of the folks back home. My expectations were high.

Congress is set up to take care of the members *only*. Wives are accommodated to a certain extent, but on the whole, wives are dispensable. If a wife goes on a junket with her husband, the federal government cannot pay her way. I was sorely disappointed to find my husband going on overseas trips without me; most of the time we couldn't afford the extra ticket. I found myself staying at home with the children, coordinating and planning our social schedule and various meetings, answering mail, and feeling resentful. Bob would dash in with an overflowing suitcase of dirty clothes, expected at the Capitol early the next morning. We had many heated conversations that ended abruptly when Bob ran out of the house, late for some committee meeting. I think it's safe to say that similar scenes were enacted all over the city by other congressional families.

Despite these annoyances, life was good in Georgetown. We loved our house. Built around 1850, it had been well preserved, but it was modernized enough to be comfortable. The children carried keys to the basement door, which entered into a hall that held bicycles, gloves, hats, and boots for easy access. Willie came and went the most; he had immediately procured a paper route for the *Washington Post.*

A neighbor later told me that, in Georgetown, people didn't generally get to know their neighbors until after about thirty years, but Willie soon became our ambassador to the neighborhood. He shoveled snow off porches for Georgetown widows and delivered papers daily. Not long after we arrived, Bob went to the Georgetown Pharmacy, which was owned by a wonderful man everyone called Doc, to cash a check. As Bob gave Doc his credentials, Doc said, "Oh yes, you're Willie's father."

CONGRESS, ITSELF

Both houses of Congress are like clubs, and each has its own wives' club. New members of Congress are immediately schooled in the ways of the institution and the rules of the system so they will know how to comport themselves on the floor of the House or Senate. The long, hard road to Congress is rewarded by instant acceptance into the most elite club in the country. After enduring years of campaigning, raising money, and being a politician, you then reap the benefits of becoming a member of the U.S. Congress.

Congress is made up of ordinary men with inflated egos, whose members are constantly striving to maintain balance and avoid the inevitable egomania, which can kill a political career if left unchecked. The institution itself contributes to the inflating of egos. Elevator operators must know members by sight; they hold the elevator for members only, while others are left waiting. Members have a private gym with a swimming pool in the Capitol.

They get their haircuts at a cut rate in the Capitol Barber Shop. A television studio is provided for members to make tapes touting their accomplishments to be viewed by their constituents in their home districts on the local evening news. Along with full health insurance, they have the convenience of an on-site doctor, consulted often for ailments like the sniffles, and the Bethesda Naval Hospital is available for more serious health problems. Congressmen get preferential treatment from their staffs, families, and constituents—the world. But they (and their families) pay a price: members can become insulated and isolated from the realities of life and lose contact with their constituencies. The insulation of politicians on any level of government poses a danger to the republic; this subject has been addressed by many concerned historians. George Reedy, who was President Johnson's national press secretary for years, was so concerned about the increasing insulation of our presidents that he wrote a book about it, *The Twilight of the Presidency.* Even less-powerful and less-visible congressmen can become sheltered megalomaniacs. When Bob came home in the evening acting authoritative, as if he were still at the office, I would remind him that he was *not* "the Congressman" at home; he was simply Bob. Congressional families can suffer from benign neglect on all sides, and when congressmen become overbearingly arrogant, it's sometimes easier for children and wives to distance themselves than to deal with them.

Although members of Congress have many perks, there are definite downsides to the job. It demands long hours in and out of their offices, meeting constituents, running to the House or Senate floor to cast a vote, attending committee meetings for hours, and attending special receptions before going home in the evening. Fund-raising is a constant concern in order to raise enough money to wage a campaign in the next election. Unless a member is dedicated to a healthy lifestyle, they become overweight from eating too much of the wrong food, sitting too much, and drinking too much alcohol. Bob rode his bicycle to the Capitol, rode horses when in Texas, and walked a lot, which kept him in overall good shape, but on the whole, Congress is a very unhealthy place. In view of the stress and constant pace, it's little wonder that many members in the late sixties were alcoholic. There was booze everywhere. Alcoholism wasn't discussed much during that era, but people drank *a lot*. Bob, I soon found out, was a "functional alcoholic"—he didn't drink until 5 p.m., but then he slugged down two or three doubles in the office and moseyed over to a reception to drink and graze at some lobbyist's invitation.

JUNKETS: THE PERK THAT ALMOST MAKES IT WORTH IT

Junkets were arranged in conjunction with other governments to facilitate the exchange of ideas and trade among nations. Meetings and briefings were set up, arranged by the Pentagon because the level of organization required military precision. I went on a few junkets when we could afford it during the years I spent in Washington from 1967–1973 when married to Bob. The itineraries included tours to see the country and meet with heads of state and government officials which members could attend by choice. Photo ops abounded during these meetings and publicity shots were handed to the members at the end of the trip.

Members and their wives or husbands were flown in comfort on Air Force One or Two—Delta or American's version of first-class paled in comparison. Eggs Benedict and a drink were placed in your hand any time you even *looked* like you wanted something. Everything had been thought of, down to the last sumptuous detail. Gambling was the favorite in-flight pastime. Bob said that on one trip a guy played poker all the way to England, got off the plane to see a horse race, and then got right back on to play poker the entire way back. Members would sign up for a junket, fly free to the first destination, bid adios to the crew, sojourn at their leisure, and pay one-way passage back to the United States.

From notes I made in 1975, on a junket to Italy:

August 2 1975, 5:30 a.m. A nice, bright-eyed young man waits across the street with the car trunk open, eager to carry the luggage and deliver bodies to Andrews Air Force Base, where we board a V-137 for Rome. The car radio crackles with the voices of various other bright-eyed young men who have been dispatched to other parts of the city to fetch other congressmen and their wives. Someone has evidently lost a representative named "Ashe." He isn't where he is supposed to be; "please spell that name over again," comes the searching voice of whoever is in charge of delivering Rep. What's His Name. The V.I.P. lounge at Andrews is appointed with smiling stewardesses at 5:30 a.m. who either 1) didn't sleep all night in order to preserve their hairdos or 2) got up at 3:00 a.m. to fix them. Doilies decorate the coffee layout.

In straggle the other members of the departing party, mostly a Republican group. These are men and women from North Carolina, West Virginia. The men are in plaid double-knit polyester suits; wives in either "smart pantsuits" or suitable attire for Chamber of Commerce-type meetings: skirt, blouse, matching earrings. Everyone greets everyone else with fraternal jocularity, as if they need each other's vote.

The military is marvelous. I wonder what they think of all these Congressmen who look like guys who sell insurance or shoes. They snap to attention and really seem to enjoy their job, greeting each other with boy-scout clichés. The legislative liaison man in charge of the group says, "We don't have to do anything but enjoy ourselves." He knows just how to handle all these egos.

We're trotted out to the plane. The official photographer takes pictures of us boarding. The plane is super-comfortable. You will not encounter any glamour among this group. No Kennedy or Johnson slickness. It's sort of nice; Republicans are so middle-America.

Junkets are a prime example of the special treatment afforded our nationally elected officials. And political analysts wonder whether or not this special treatment further insulates our government officials from the reality of their constituents' lives? I think the answer is obvious.

THE CONGRESSIONAL SOCIAL WHIRL

In the first three months of 1967, Bob and I attended at least twenty social occasions sponsored by lobbying groups ranging from bankers to seafarers, and made two trips to Texas to attend political functions. This was in addition to the general congressional social circuit: for me it was teas, luncheons, style shows, and receptions, while Bob had breakfasts, lunch meetings, and evening receptions. From the get-go we received invitations from associations we'd never heard of. Bob's staff wanted him to attend lobby functions to keep abreast of legislative issues affecting his district, so we dutifully trotted off to these affairs. At first, I had a good time, but the whole routine quickly became a mundane nuisance: arranging dinner for the children; dressing up; picking up Bob on the Hill; driving to X, Y, or Z hotel; drinking wine and eating Swedish meatballs and/or pastry shells filled with something unidentifiable. "It's good to develop a healthy ingratitude toward the lobby," Bob used to say, and he was right.

Lobbyists have often elicited negative reactions but I knew them as people who were simply trying to get their point across to legislators. Frank "Posh" Oltorf, my lobbyist friend for Brown & Root of Houston, was the only lobbyist I knew personally. He was a friend of Lyndon's and later wrote *The Marlin Compound* about his family in Marlin, Texas. But this predates the super-lobby of the nineties and the purchase of the government by the corporate world. This is perhaps an overstatement, for there are, I would like to think, some members of Congress who still have the common good of the people in mind when they vote. But now more than ever there seems to be a disconnect between the people and our elected representatives, and a connection between the corporate world and the paid-for representative. This unfortunate situation has become more egregious and will probably endure as long as such small percentages of the electorate vote. Corporate America has the money and power to make huge campaign contributions that far outweigh individual contributions, and consequently the will of the people is diluted.

In 1967, Bob was fifty-four; I was thirty-six. We were energetic and wanted to do the right thing—we wanted to do it all. We socialized diligently. Most people didn't know how to throw a good party, but President Johnson and Lady Bird were masters of a good time. They knew the essential ingredients: good food, good drink, good music, and an attentive host and hostess. LBJ was the best lobbyist of all. At every party he lobbied every member of Congress and kissed every wife.

At one party early on, I was standing talking to Bob when I felt someone walk up behind me and press his whole body against mine. I knew instantly who it was. Lyndon said, "You act like you like that guy you're with." Then he hugged me and invited us to travel to Texas the next day. I explained that we had a two-year-old at home, and he said, "We're gonna have to fix you up with some of those things we send to India to keep 'em from having so many kids." I had reconnected with the Johnsons, yet they never mentioned my previous incarnation as a twenty-five-year-old secretary married to Bill Brammer. Nor did I.

The president was not so different from the LBJ I had worked for in the 1950s. In a letter to my parents dated March 1, 1967, I wrote, "Had a divine time at the White House. In fact, had such a good time, we were the last to leave. The President and Lady Bird were very cordial and hospitable. Of course I renewed old acquaintances and my jaw was sore the next day from talking. The best thing that happened was that Vice President Humphrey promised Bob that he could fly to Houston with him on a visit, 'provided you bring your wife.'"

Life was exciting and busy. I was constantly on the phone with Bob's staff, coordinating social and political functions, answering letters, and arranging "eat-ins" at the office for the staff and visiting constituents. Bob had a great staff who were fun. We'd sit around the big oval table that Bob used as a desk, laughing and talking and drinking wine, discussing politics and occasionally coming up with a good idea to further Bob's political interests. These sessions were good for Bob for he had a tendency to close himself off from people.

There was much socializing surrounding the Johnson administration because there were so many Texans who knew each other in Washington. Jack and Mary Margaret Valenti were part of Lyndon's White House inner circle. Later, Jack became president of the Motion Picture Association of America, a job for which he was perfectly matched. Friends were happy they remained in D.C. and congressional families looked forward to evenings in the new commodious MPAA building watching a movie and socializing at Jack's invitation. Jack was quoted in the Sunday Washington Star News in 1973 saying I was one of his favorite dinner partners. That meant a lot to me, for Jack was a rare individual who elevated the mood and the conversation in any gathering.

Another reason there was so much socializing was that LBJ liked to party and was a pretty good dancer. At one point, in 1968, we flew on Air Force One with the president and members of the Texas delegation and their wives to dine and dance in Austin in honor of the president, and flew back to D.C. the same night in an alcohol-soaked time warp. There were small, chic dinners with our Georgetown neighbors, who introduced us to national journalists and other congressmen and their wives. I felt very comfortable being back in Washington. My children were in good public schools. Bob's daughters were ensconced at the University of Pennsylvania. Bob and I were operating optimally. We loved our house and had fun exploring antique stores in Maryland and Virginia for treasures. I was happy.

A FRONT-ROW SEAT TO A REVOLUTION

On April 4, 1968, a spring night, Bob brought home Ronnie Dugger, editor of the *Texas Observer,* to have dinner and talk politics.

We discussed the Vietnam War, as we often did, moving back and forth between the kitchen and the dining room. Like a low-grade fever, the war had been with the American people for several years. We spoke of the inhumanity and hopelessness of the situation, and how President Johnson was mistaken in thinking it was winnable. The evening was interrupted by the tragic news of Reverend Martin Luther King's assassination. We sat in utter disbelief, watching cities across the nation erupt almost immediately into riots and looting. Southeast D.C. was on fire—we could see the smoke from our backyard in Georgetown. Bob frantically installed a bolt on our front door so it couldn't be kicked open. Simultaneously, anti-war demonstrations were taking place on Wisconsin Avenue and M Street. I empathized with the protesters, but the hysteria was unsettling, even though our house remained untouched. The civil rights and anti-war movements had come together and exploded.

The civil rights dilemma had been going on far too long for patience, in spite of the fact that Johnson had done more than any other president for civil rights, working first with Dr. King to stem the growing unrest. When King was killed, he had been in the process of organizing a Poor People's Campaign march to Washington to bring attention to the poverty problems of all races. His fellow minister, Reverend Ralph Abernathy, carried on the organizing of what became known as "Resurrection City." President Johnson met with Abernathy and made sure our government cooperated in arranging the accommodations to be set up for the people living and sleeping on the National Mall in protest. Dr. King's assassination sparked a march of poor people to go to Washington from all over the nation.

John Hill, the dean of the School of Architecture at the University of Maryland and a friend of ours, helped prepare for the masses of people heading toward D.C. John invited Bob and me to tour the Mall area to see the plywood "tents" his students had designed to house the people in Resurrection City. It was a beautiful May day. Suddenly, as we admired the structures, we found ourselves surrounded by about twenty young black men with big 'fros—they were the "marshals" on the site and had heard that there was a congressman on the premises. They began to shout at Bob, who was holding our three-year-old, Sarah; we were encircled and couldn't walk away. Bob tried to tell them he'd supported their causes throughout his political career, but the men were so full of anger at Congress and the government in general that they weren't going to let a live one go. A man in a Malcolm X T-shirt was really giving Bob hell, so I screamed at him, "Stop giving this man shit! You don't know what you're talking about!" That got his attention, and he said to Bob, "I can't talk to you, but I can talk to your woman." Then he guided me to a tent where I could sign up as a volunteer, and we were allowed to move on peacefully. Bob was amused that I could speak in language that could get through to the man.

The next day I received a call from a woman named Cheryl Robinson, who identified herself as the wife of Ray Robinson, the man in the Malcolm X shirt. She invited me over to their tent for barbecued chicken, asking me specifically not to bring my husband. The next day my daughter, Shelby; Victor Emmanuel, a Harvard student (and avid bird-watcher who later founded a successful birding tour business); and I drove to the tent city on the Mall. It was a beautiful spring day and we heard music as we made our way through the maze of tents. Cheryl had given me good directions and barbecued chicken on a grill provided welcoming smells. Cheryl, to my surprise, was white. Ray and Cheryl Robinson were like any young couple who were excitedly fixing up their new "home." We were introduced to their baby daughter Desiree. Ray offered us a beer and we talked. They had lived in Germany and were actively involved in poverty issues. Cheryl was smart and informed, and we had good conversation about the women's movement and the inequalities between men and women. Ray was in agreement with her views and during the conversation looked me in the eye and said "Don't you know you're a nigger too?" Ray Robinson definitely got my attention and his words resonated with me long after our visit.

Slowly, buses arrived from all over the nation. Resurrection City filled with poor people attempting to bring their plight to the government's attention. The atmosphere started out fun enough, like a huge campout: a mess tent, portable toilets, people playing music and having a good time.

But then the rains started, and they didn't stop for almost a month. The wooden structures warped and leaked. Feeding the hundreds of people became an overwhelming task for the organizers. The place was a mess. I collected cots, blankets, and any other supplies I could get using whatever clout I had as a congressional wife. Shelby and I cooked huge pots of beans. Hygiene became a problem, and I opened our house to folks needing showers. The Robinsons were in touch by phone on a daily basis.

Then, as if all this weren't enough, anti-war demonstrations began to spread out over the city, and troops shot tear gas everywhere. We put up a sign in front of our house inviting people inside to rinse out their eyes. We could hear the rioting on Wisconsin Avenue and M Street and the police and National Guard sirens. Students from all over the country congregated in Georgetown to be close to the action. During the day, after the debris from the previous night's rioting had been cleared away, young people appeared on Wisconsin Avenue selling handicrafts and acting as a visual presence against the war.

Students at Western High School, Sidney's school, set the school on fire six times in one week. General chaos in the city had set off the anger of black students who were bussed to the Georgetown schools—they weren't emotionally invested in the neighborhood, and they were justifiably enraged, so they acted out. Sidney was a conscientious student, so when she started talking about staying home and studying, I realized that the situation was getting serious. We decided to send her to a private school in Maryland. All four children had been enrolled in public schools, and having to switch to private was a hard choice, because we believed deeply in the public school system. But bussing wasn't working for the benefit of all the students. One by one our children ended up in private schools.

A CULTURE IN TURMOIL

When deep cultural changes do not get expressed politically, there are repercussions. President Johnson was a Texas "big daddy" who wanted to believe that he would be able to deliver not only relief to the poor and civil rights to blacks but also a victory to the South Vietnamese. But Johnson was not able to understand the depth of the cultural changes taking place. By the late sixties the country was prosperous, and people found themselves able to think about themselves as individuals—unique human beings with specific sets of choices, anxieties, and experiences. Everyone wanted to be free to individuate. Men and women began to sleep and travel together, racially mixed or not.

The spiritual revolution, which opened the western mind to eastern thought, was yet another aspect of the widening breach between the older and younger generations. Hinduism and Buddhism offered young people who were searching for meaning in their lives a new path that other religions couldn't—and war and killing didn't make sense in this school of thought. Experimental drugs exacerbated the breach. Educators like Richard Alpert and Timothy Leary explored lysergic acid and wrote about how it united them with universal consciousness; drugs were a way to temporarily connect with the higher self. The older generation and, more importantly, President Johnson, couldn't seem to comprehend these massive shifts.

Not surprisingly, Johnson seemed sad and tired. He had received many threats on his life, and the disapproval of thousands of young and not-so-young Americans was clear. It is painful to watch footage of LBJ from this time in meetings with advisors—his head bowed, his body contorted in an attitude of defeat and sorrow as he strove for a solution. He was used to winning, but this time he just couldn't deliver. The war could not be won. As a parent with a front-row seat to these events, I empathized with both the young *and* the old. The leaders of our country seemed like parents unwilling to open their minds to the views of the younger generation. Bob and I felt extremely conflicted. Although our allegiance was to President Johnson, we desperately wanted him to stop the war.

On June 11, 1968, Bob and I attended a dinner at the White House honoring the Shah of Iran. Because of my mixed emotions about the war and the president, I wasn't thrilled about going, but my mood was elevated a bit by the Strolling Strings, the group of Air Force violinists who often played at White House dinners. We were seated at round tables accommodating about six; I was seated next to the president and across from Margaret Truman. Johnson was mellow and relaxed. I didn't have the nerve to confront him about the war, but I did speak to him about Resurrection City, painting a picture of my experiences there. Johnson said, "Those people out there are electing Richard Nixon right now." He also described the hundreds of death threats against him and told me that he yearned to get back to Texas and spend time with his grandchildren.

By late June, the quagmire on the National Mall that was Resurrection City had been shut down by the authorities. The Robinson family and their group camped on some open land in Fairfax County, Virginia, for a few weeks. I took the kids for a visit one day, and as we drove away I was stopped by a county police officer. My car had congressional license plates on it, but I was asked to verify its ownership. Upset that we were being watched by the authorities, Bob complained to the Fairfax County chief of police, who explained the incident away as a "routine check." (Later, a benefactor gave the Robinsons and their group ten acres of land in Alabama. The last letter I received, dated 1971, said, "We raise goats, chickens, ducks, hogs, and rabbits. This year we harvested one ton of sweet potatoes and canned over three hundred jars of butter beans, blackberries, squash, and other garden vegetables. Soybeans and field corn will be harvested soon. We are revolutionary farmers.")

Resurrection City, the assassinations of Dr. King and later, Senator Robert Kennedy, and the looting and burning of major American cities had all taken place in the span of only a few months. We thought the nation was falling apart.

The anti-war movement spawned an anti-war presidential candidate, and in late 1967, Senator Eugene McCarthy entered the

1968 presidential race as an alternative to the increasingly vulnerable President Johnson. McCarthy won the New Hampshire primary and by March of 1968 President Johnson decided not to seek reelection. McCarthy seemed to have a calming effect on the outraged youth. Senator Robert Kennedy, Johnson's nemesis, also announced that he was running. Tragically, of course, his was a short-lived campaign, so in the end it was Senator McCarthy and Hubert Humphrey vying for the nomination. McCarthy, who was erudite and handsome, with a good sense of humor, had the support of the youth and those who had supported Bobby Kennedy.

A giant rally in Houston had been scheduled, at which McCarthy was to be publicly endorsed by the liberal leaders of Texas. Bob and I flew to Houston with McCarthy and checked into the Rice Hotel. We were to meet him later in his suite. From my notes:

> Eugene was resting. We watched a TV interview that had been taped of him earlier on the room set with two of his aides, his secretary, and a young man. Eugene came in dressed in fresh clothes, looking good. We all had a drink and sat and talked for about thirty minutes. Left the Rice. Bob, Eugene, and Ralph Yarborough were hustled into a car and sped away. I was left on the curb wondering how in hell was I going to get to Hermann Park. I jumped into a press car and rode to Hermann Park with Sam Somebody from *Life* magazine. There was a huge crowd but I managed to join Bob onstage while the speeches and cheering went on. After the rally the Secret Service guys herded us off the stage toward the waiting cars. Once again they pushed the three men into a car and slammed the door and took off. I ran to the car behind them, opened the back door, and jumped in. I thought it was a press car, but it turned out to be a Secret Service car—the two men in the front seat were furious at me for jumping in their car. I wouldn't get out. Almost immediately a voice came over the radio telling them that I was a wife. Going fast, following Eugene's limo to Astrodome. Joined Bob, Ralph,

and Eugene while they watched the last inning of a ball game. Eugene was a big baseball fan. The Secret Service men were nice and apologized for giving me a hard time.

After so much turmoil, why were we surprised at what transpired at the Chicago Democratic Convention? But we were. The nation watched in horror as police billy-clubbed and tear-gassed young kids. My children sympathized with the demonstrators, and so did I. There was no doubt about it now, the populace was polarized: hawks against doves. Jim Rowe, an advisor to President Johnson, and I had lunch occasionally to discuss the war. He was a hawk; he'd try to explain the various reasons why we had to stay in the war. I would give him my argument that the passion driving the North Vietnamese was stronger than our military hardware. Years later, in the late seventies, Rowe complimented me with the admission that I had seen the realities of the war before he did.

A MORE PERSONAL REVOLUTION

The calamitous year had brought about profound changes and my children and I were all experiencing them. Sidney and Shelby were now seventeen and fifteen, and I discussed sexual freedom and contraception with them, "just in case." Perched on the cusp between the generations of the fifties and the sixties, my mentality reflected a heightened awareness of the growing sexual permissiveness of the times.

I enjoyed flirting with men I found attractive, and in several instances the flirtation led to one-night stands or short-term flings. How I had the time and energy to arrange these is beyond me—I can only conclude that they were the result of the volatile combination of an enormous amount of energy, raging hormones, and a deep insecurity.

Like most men who have extramarital affairs, I never let the situation interfere with my duties at home; I wasn't *that* self-destructive.

My default assumption was that men would cheat on their wives if they had the chance, and I still think that holds true for the majority. As a fifties girl who desperately wanted to appear perfect, the sexual revolution in the sixties was a long-awaited panacea, and it fed my sense of freedom. But even so, I was careful to protect the status quo.

THE SEVENTIES: CHANGES, BOTH PUBLIC AND PRIVATE

President Johnson's remark about Resurrection City, that "those people out there are electing Richard Nixon right now," turned out to be prophetic. The backlash against the violence and rebellion of those who opposed the war won out, and Richard Nixon defeated Vice President Hubert Humphrey in the 1968 presidential election. You could tell the Republicans were in town because of the influx of gray heads.

If you judge an administration by its soirees, the Nixon presidency was an utter failure. The Nixon functions were uninspired and dull, particularly compared to the great parties of the LBJ administration. Before one White House party, Willie asked me to get Nixon's autograph for his collection. Bob and I stood in line in the East Room for what seemed like forever. Waiters brought drinks; everyone in line was a little tipsy. When we entered the next room, there in a tight group were the Nixons and the Agnews, all lit up and in full makeup, standing in a creepy tableau as if they were wax dummies. Later, I introduced myself to Pat Nixon, who was much prettier and friendlier than her public persona conveyed, and asked her for the autograph. She took me by the arm and led me over to the president, who was in the middle of a conversation with Barry Goldwater. Nixon graciously introduced me to Senator

Goldwater and signed a paper for Willie, but there was no charisma or excitement in meeting the president; he was just doing his duty, as was I.

MORE CHANGES AND A GROWING DISTANCE

When I try to remember Bob during this time, I can't. The disconnect between us was increasing. I was making friends with younger people, and Bob was consumed by his role in the political realm. One of my new friends was a psychiatrist who knew both Bob and me, and I asked him for counsel about my feelings of resentment toward my husband. He asked me what I did during the day, from the moment I woke up. I told him that first, I looked at my daybook to see where Bob was supposed to be. He said, "Why? Isn't he capable of keeping up with his schedule?" My answer was no. The psychiatrist recommended that I stop doing so much for Bob and start doing some things for myself.

Objectively, it probably seemed like I was on top of the world. I enjoyed socializing. We had homes in Houston and Georgetown. My children were growing up in the enriched cultural environment of Washington, D.C. My husband was doing well politically, having been named the most outstanding new member in his first term. He was put on the House Science and Astronautics Committee which was good for its connection to the National Air and Space Agency. NASA's manned spacecraft center was bringing new industries and jobs into Houston. He was also fulfilling speaking engagements and going on junkets. Why couldn't I be a committed wife and grow fat and comfortable and look forward to retiring in Houston?

A part of me wanted very much for all of this to come to pass: I would continue with the marriage, going about the work of supporting Bob in his job of representing the folks of the 8th congressional district of Texas. Then there was the part of me that was enthralled by the sixties zeitgeist. I wanted out of marriage and to express myself and to become a more individualized, independent woman. I identified with what I was reading and seeing of the women's movement. I remembered Ray Robinson's comment: "Don't you know you're a nigger too?" I read Betty Friedan's *The Feminine Mystique.* I went to a luncheon at the Democratic Women's Club to hear Gloria Steinem speak. She was tall and beautiful and looked so amazing in her short purple outfit, with those long legs and that unbelievable hair. She personified the new woman and I envied and admired her. What did I want? What I had wanted when I married Bill Brammer in 1950—to have both freedom and security. I was working hard and feeling empty, again.

My role in Bob's political life was confusing for constituents, friends, and staff. I made decisions when the staff couldn't get an answer from Bob. I remembered the names of the people who were key to his success and entertained constituents. Bob was a wonderful legislative technician, and he loved that part of the job, but he didn't take to the nitty-gritty of politics, which involved constantly dealing with people. I wanted him to look good in the eyes of his constituents, and he did, with much prodding from his staff and me. I wanted him to be more organized and independent. He couldn't change. I lost patience with his helplessness and after years of being a wife/staffer, I lost respect for him. Actually, it was more complicated than that. I was losing respect for myself for putting myself in such a position, and I wanted to free myself. Molly Ivins, who knew Bob well, wrote, "He had great charm and a very interesting mind. He was absolutely not worth dog on any kind of practical aspect of life. If Bob had not been taken care of by good women all his life, he'd have been totally nonfunctional."

I decided to take my psychiatrist friend's advice. I signed up for a course at Georgetown University on U.S. foreign policy. I had always wanted to complete my degree in government, and this would be a start. It was something just for me; Bob and the children would have to pick up the slack a bit and help with the housecleaning and cooking. They would have to get used to my being a student.

The course I took was graduate-level—even though I didn't have an undergraduate degree, my experience in politics and government was considered enough of a prerequisite. Since we were living through the Nixon administration, I chose to write a paper on rapprochement with China, which hadn't yet occurred. After researching the history of relations between the United States and China, I learned that former U.S. diplomat Averell Harriman had been Franklin Roosevelt's choice to travel to China and determine the truth of the situation.

Mr. Harriman lived just a few blocks from our house, so I called to ask him some questions. He was gracious and candid. I spent several summer afternoons at his house taking notes about his recollections and listening to his prognostications about our future with China. He seemed lonely—he started calling in the morning to discuss what was in the *Post* that day, and to ask if I'd like to join him for a swim. I usually declined, saying that I had a six-year-old daughter, but he would say, "Bring her too." (This was before Pamela Churchill Hayward reentered his life and became Mrs. Harriman.) His generosity with his memories lent my little paper a cachet it wouldn't have otherwise had. I enjoyed the class and re-enrolled the next semester.

As I began to detach myself from Bob's schedule, my world centered more around our Georgetown neighbors and Georgetown University. Ann and David Brinkley, famous news anchor for NBC, were divorcing; Ann bought the house next door and she and I became close friends. She was a D.C. native and had been a journalist for one of the wire services when she met and married David. A pretty brunette, Ann created beautiful homes and gave parties that weren't to be missed. Ann's brother, Norman Fischer, had married Cile Ragland, a friend of mine from Sweetwater, Texas, and they were living in Washington as well.

Somewhere in the back of my mind, I began to realize that I would eventually leave my marriage with Bob. But I wasn't consciously aware of it at the time. Just before the Georgetown semester started, I took a hard look at my house, which showed the signs of my neglect from the past semester. I thought about our social obligations, school clothes to shop for, Sarah's birthday party, the numerous chores that needed doing—the list went on and on. Overwhelmed, I walked to the registrar's office and withdrew from the fall semester. That night, when I told Bob what I had done, he was delighted. I cried. He didn't understand.

MULTIPLE ROLES, MANY FACES

The Vietnam War dragged on into 1971. Nixon and Kissinger *et al* didn't seem to be able to extricate us. Demonstrations grew in both size and scope; it seemed the whole country was against the war now. I went to a demonstration with my children one morning near Key Bridge, and we were aggressively confronted by soldiers. For the first time I felt really afraid. I was committed to attend a White House luncheon at the invitation of Pat Nixon later on that day, and I made it home from the demonstration just in time to get dressed. As I sat in the rarefied atmosphere of the White House, I realized once again how schizophrenic my reality was. I was playing too many roles.

Bob's secretary, Fran Gray, knew I was interested in the war, so she let me know that Congresswoman Bella Abzug had arranged a meeting for members to listen to Daniel Ellsberg talk about the war. Ellsberg had been employed at the State Department, the Department of Defense, and the Rand Corporation, where he worked on the study that eventually became known as the Pentagon Papers. He *pleaded* with the members of Congress to do something about the war. He talked and talked; it was heart-wrenching. I couldn't stand it anymore, so I raised my hand and said that while I appreciated what he was saying, I had watched the members of Congress who wanted out of Vietnam do everything they possibly could, and it was my opinion that it would take some event outside of Congress to get us out of Vietnam. Ellsberg wanted to talk after the meeting, so Bob and I convened with Ellsberg, along with Vinny McGee, a friend of Ellsberg's who was working with Businessmen for Peace, at our house in Georgetown and talked until late in the night. Ellsberg spoke eloquently about the Pentagon Papers and his willingness to risk being thrown in jail to end the war.

The next day, Vinny called. After our talk the night before, he and Daniel had walked to the corner of N and Wisconsin to hail a cab. A car had pulled up next to them, and someone had thrown acid in Daniel's face. We learned that Daniel had been under heavy surveillance for a very long time. Within a few days the world was informed by the *New York Times* that Daniel Ellsberg had released the Pentagon Papers. It was a watershed moment in the history of the Vietnam War; the papers revealed the shocking gap between what the government was feeding the public and what was actually occurring in Vietnam.

REEFER MADNESS

"Be careful, Nadine. There're Mexicans out there high on marijuana, and there's no telling what they'll do." This is a direct quote from my parents from my teenage years, usually uttered as my date and I departed for Reynosa to dance and drink. Prior to the seventies, my only experience with marijuana had been in Texas in 1963, just after I married Bob, when my friend Terellita and her boyfriend gave me a marijuana cookie to eat with my coffee for breakfast. We were laughing hysterically when the phone rang. It was Bob, telling me he needed to be picked up in Spring, a small town about four miles away; his train had had an accident. I told him we would be there in a few minutes, and then promptly forgot all about it. What seemed like hours later, Terellita said, "Didn't Bob call you about going to get him?" We rushed around frantically and drove ten miles an hour to Spring, giggling all the way.

I didn't try smoking marijuana until years later, when some of my Georgetown neighbors offered it up. Initially I demurred, but eventually, when the situation presented itself with a married couple with whom I felt comfortable, I took the plunge. The first few times I was wound so tight I couldn't feel the effects, but I soon learned to relax and enjoy the present. I was slowing down and becoming more aware of my environment. My life began to reflect this slower pace and heightened awareness. I became more health-conscious. I quit drinking alcohol and started practicing yoga—Ann Brinkley and I went to class twice a week. I began to make my own yogurt. A weekly farmer's market was held at a church nearby, where I bought fresh vegetables and dairy products for my family.

It didn't take long before I realized how hypocritical I had been in the past about condemning those who smoked marijuana. Marijuana alters our consciousness and makes us more aware; alcohol results in a sugar rush which can make us more active and aggressive. My parents didn't drink but they weren't intolerant of those who did. None of my relatives drank alcohol. It was a given in the fifties and sixties. I drank it socially and if I drank too much, I got a headache. In Washington and Austin we knew who drank to excess and avoided them. Bill Brammer liked amphetamines so he could stay awake for long periods of time. Bob Eckhardt drank a lot of alcohol. The first thing he did when arriving home in the evening was pour a big drink and have several before dinner. I went to bed before he did, leaving him smoking his cigar with a glass of brandy. One morning I found him lying on the floor in his suit where he had passed out in the basement. It frightened me and I confided in Ann Brinkley. She recommended I call a friend of hers who was in Alcoholics Anonymous. He asked me if Bob drank more than eight ounces of alcohol per day. I had to laugh. He asked me if I thought Bob would attend Alcoholics Anonymous. If he wouldn't, he advised me to wait until he was sober and tell him I would leave him and take Sarah if he didn't quit drinking. I followed his instruction, and Bob agreed that he drank too much and promised he would drink fruit juice instead. That lasted a few days. He couldn't help it; he had the disease. He had had it all the way back when his father would go searching for him and find him passed out in the neighbors' yards. He was a mellow drunk and loved to laugh and tell stories. However, he flew off the handle at minor irritants, yelling and screaming in fits of anger—common alcoholic responses. The more I avoided drinking alcohol, the further I moved away from him emotionally. The more I changed, in this way and in others, the more I became estranged from Bob's activities. Spending time with Georgetown students who were discussing the war, Eastern philosophy, and feminism stimulated and excited me, for I was learning from them what I couldn't from my peer group.

Georgetown was a rich ghetto in the late sixties and early seventies. There was always action on the street, people sitting on front stoops just hanging out. I noticed that an apartment several doors down was especially active—music continually poured from the windows, usually the Stones not getting any satisfaction or Santana singing about gypsy women, and a big hookah sat on a table in the large bay window. I could see a hammock hanging in the living room. The smell of pot wafted from the place. Soon I got to know its residents: George, Mickey, and Shorty.

They invited me to tea. I arrived to Chuck Berry's "Nadine" blaring on the stereo. We drank tea and smoked a joint; they said they enjoyed my company and wanted to trip with me, but didn't want me to get in any trouble because of my husband's position. We were fast friends from then on, always coming in and out of each other's houses. They socialized with my family, teasing seven-year-old Sarah, who loved it, and horsing around with Willie, who was fourteen and running the streets.

George, who was half Greek and half Danish, and I were instantly attracted to each other. The sexual tension ramped up until finally we acted on it. He graduated shortly thereafter and left the city, but he always wrote to me and returned to visit. The relationship endured for years, intermittently, and I value the experience. I loved the way the consciousness of the younger men of that era had been raised about women—their concern about our feelings and sexual satisfaction was very much apparent. In just fifteen years men had evolved from those of my generation—who became their job and avoided discussing their feelings and never asked their wives how they felt about sex, money, or anything else—to an entirely different kind of man. Many of my female contemporaries lived with or married younger men after their divorces. My female friends and I have often pondered our fates since that time when we experienced the gentler, idealistic, spiritual young men we knew and loved during their twenties and our forties.

Ironically enough, I had a lot of fun during those years, even though my marriage was failing and Nixon was in office. Perhaps it was a relief from the intensity and involvement with the Johnson administration—I had a chance to focus on other things. I was having fun visiting places Bob would never go, such as the Cellar Door, a club a few blocks away from our house, to hear Miles Davis and the Modern Jazz Quartet, and doing things he didn't like to do. Emotionally, I had moved even further away from him. This bothered his staff, because it was in their interest to keep him in office. The pattern was to push on me to push on him, because otherwise he drifted and lost contact with his district. It was in my interest, too, to keep him in office, since neither of us wanted to dismantle what we'd built. It worked so well on the outside, why couldn't it work on the inside? Neither one of us could look inward for the answers. We ran from our feelings and filled our lives with other people. Maintaining the facade was easier when we were doing work connected with the office. Bob enjoyed being a congressman; he had seniority by now. He gained a reputation for his objectivity and ability to write legislation and championed consumer rights. We had an unspoken conspiracy; I would help him at election time, but would cut back on the day-to-day work, and this way we'd make an attempt at maintaining the status quo.

BILL MAKES AN APPEARANCE

So much was going on in D.C. that I hadn't paid much attention to Bill's whereabouts. He had worked for a while in 1966 for Hemisfair in San Antonio, an effort spearheaded by businessmen and politicians to promote enterprise between Texas and Mexico by building a permanent exhibition area in San Antonio. We heard through the grapevine that he and Dorothy were in California, then Colorado, and then, in 1969, that they had separated. Soon after, Jay Milner hired Bill to teach a journalism course at Southern Methodist University in Dallas. Bill had always been at the vanguard of new thought, and friends applauded his SMU job; it was hopeful news that he had employment as a respected writer. Jody Gent, at that time the wife of Peter Gent, the Dallas Cowboy, who would later write *North Dallas Forty* and at the time was teaching advertising in the journalism department, said, "Bill turned forty living off Oaklawn in Big D with two students—a poet and a dance major—while teaching creative writing with a highlighter and *Rolling Stone* magazine. And he used ours because he didn't even have a subscription." In 1971, Bill contacted us and said he wanted to see the children. He hadn't seen them for at least four years. Sidney had graduated from the Canterbury School in southern Maryland and was working for Senator Ralph Yarborough of Texas before going to college. Shelby was about to graduate from Holy Trinity High School in Georgetown, and Willie was an accomplished young magician who worked in Al's Magic Shop on Pennsylvania Avenue after school and performed at neighborhood birthday parties.

When Bill showed up at our house, I was hospitable for the sake of the kids, who were very glad to see him despite his neglect. I was curious to lay my eyes on him, to see how he looked—he was always interesting, as he was constantly on the cutting edge of what was happening culturally. I also was hoping to see that he had pulled himself together. He said he was writer in residence at Bowling Green State University in Ohio and gave Sidney advice about writing, passing along the textbooks he had used at SMU: *The Student as Nigger,* by Jerry Farber; *Montage: Investigations in Language,* by William Sparke and Clark McKowen; and *Regarding Wave,* by Gary Snyder. Bill also invited Sidney and her boyfriend Fred for a visit. He was impressed with Willie, the young magician, and Shelby's being an aspiring young actress.

Later, Sidney and Fred decided to road-trip to Texas; they stayed a week with Bill, who by then had left Bowling Green State and returned to Dallas without finishing the semester. Sidney's impressions of the trip were in tune with the times: there was plenty of room in Bill's old house, with beans cooking in the kitchen, a lot of students, and a plentiful supply of drugs. About a week after they had visited, police busted the house and Bill was arrested. Any hopes he might have had of a teaching career were gone. Bill pled guilty to possession of marijuana in return for five years probation.

BACK HOME TO TEXAS, ONCE AGAIN

After leaving office, Lyndon Johnson did just exactly what he had told me he wanted to do: he returned to Texas to enjoy his grandchildren, and four years later, in January of 1973, at the age of only sixty-four, he died at his ranch in Johnson City. After the memorial in Washington, the whole Texas delegation was flown to the ranch for the burial. We stood in the freezing rain for what seemed like hours while eulogies were delivered and songs were sung. We all hated to see him go. Later, it was rumored that his unexpected death of a heart attack had occurred in much the same fashion and circumstance as the death of fictitious Arthur Fenstemaker who died in bed with his secretary in *Country Pleasures,* the last novella of *The Gay Place.* The final phrases read, ". . . and they all stood a short distance from the bed and looked at Arthur, pale blue in the soft light, bathed in the faint fragrance of woman, grinning over some great vague private joke."

By August of 1973 I had been a congressional wife in D.C. for six years. Note from my journal, May 4, 1973:

> I am exhausted. I am on a downer about what a superficial life we have in Washington. I'm becoming more introspective and I'm afraid the more power Bob attains, the more he is seduced by "power trip" sycophants. I want to cut out all the extraneous socializing. It's a waste of time and energy.

I missed Sidney and Shelby who were both at the University of Texas at Austin, which was expensive. Bob and I discussed my moving back to Houston to save money and have a little apartment in Washington. Willie and Sarah liked the idea. I wanted to move back to the country where I could have a garden and I could keep in touch with the 8th district for Bob, which appealed to him. Willie, Sarah, and I moved, arriving in Texas at about the same time that Nixon was indicted for his ignoble behavior. I moved back to Texas to escape from this marriage as I had with the first one; I was totally unaware of it at the time.

My life slowed to a less frenetic pace. Friends from D.C. and Austin visited, and I treated them to good weed, good food, and good political talk on our screened porch in the woods twenty-five miles north of Houston. I didn't return to D.C. for a year. When I did, it was to help Bob run for chairman of the Democratic Study Group, a group of liberal Democrats who studied legislation and determined strategies to pursue in the House. It would be only a three-week campaign. Bob wanted very much to win the chairmanship, and although we were living in different cities, once again I got my own ego involved in the race and decided to stay in Washington, going at the campaign full tilt. We had Sarah flown to D.C., where she was my constant companion, sleeping in the office, waiting for her mother and father.

There were a couple of young, smart lawyers who liked Bob's liberal politics, and they advised him to hire a more aggressive administrative assistant if he wanted the win. A young Harvard Law School grad named Ken Levine came on board, and we set up a boiler-room–type operation, from which we called members whose vote Bob needed. Using maps of members' locations, we had Bob visit their offices to ask them personally for their vote. We scheduled members for drinks with Bob in his office each afternoon; Ken and I were there to facilitate the conversations.

The campaign was short but intense, and Bob was victorious. He was the first Southerner to be chairman. Bob got the credit and recognition and power, and I got to feel needed. As unhappy as I was in the marriage, I derived just enough satisfaction from his position of power to keep me hooked in. And then there were the occasional good times, which led me to think that perhaps things weren't so bad—the ambiguity made it difficult to make a clear decision. We had an extended family for which we were the central figures, and there was so much invested in our being together. It was incredibly hard to break it up.

Back in Houston, I earned a real estate license in an effort to establish independence. I thought I could make fast money in real estate; everyone seemed to be doing it. I was motivated, as my elderly parents were frail and I was worried about them financially. My timing was poor for about that time the market started a downward slide, I began my real estate career full-time. I was working ninety hours a week and wondering why I wasn't making money. Bob came home every other weekend to relax. I couldn't entertain constituents and family because of my work schedule, but his expectations didn't seem to change. I resented his giving lip service to my efforts toward independence when his actions indicated the opposite.

Out of the blue, on my forty-fourth birthday, I got a call from my biological father, whom I had never met. He sang "Happy Birthday" and sounded personable enough on the phone. I decided to visit him in Oklahoma City on my next trip to D.C. It didn't take long to see what a lousy husband and father he was. His wife was clearly angry and unhappy and his sons seemed uneasy around him. He was, however, a good musician. My mother had not lied to me about that. I had no emotional attachment to him whatsoever, but the trip resolved my curiosity and set my mind free to better appreciate my stepfather, the one who had cared for me all my life.

THE DEATH OF A MARRIAGE

In 1975, *The Power Lovers,* a book about politicians and their marriages, was published. It was written by Myra MacPherson, a reporter for the *Washington Post* who had become a good friend of mine in D.C. The *Houston Chronicle* ran excerpts pertaining to Bob and me, portraying us as still together but implying that we were at least fifty percent hypocritical. Myra's portrayal was right; I was one angry congressional wife. The situation between Bob and me had taken a turn for the worse. Willie Morris's ex-wife, Celia, had been a friend of mine. She had been a houseguest of ours in D.C. for a few days during the summers of 1971 and 1972, and I learned that Bob was having an affair with her. The situation was becoming gossip in Houston, which could hurt Bob politically. He could lose his congressional seat, in which we both had a stake. I asked Bob to move out. I had been emotionally removed from him for a long time, and the affair with Celia just accelerated the separation and eventual divorce. We separated, ironically, when he was at the peak of his career, just as Bill and I had separated at the point when *The Gay Place* was being published. I left each marriage at the time that each husband was reaping the rewards of our mutual dedication and hard work. I didn't know how to achieve for myself, only for others, and I felt ripped off and empty. Bob got to keep the office I had helped earn—and a congressional office cannot be divvied up like pots and pans and books. In addition, Bob was having an affair with an old "friend" of mine—we had done a good job of humiliating each other in the last days of our marriage.

My state of mind was precarious. I was anxious and confused, having flashbacks to my separation from Bill, many years before. A part of me knew I had somehow put myself in this painful place, but I didn't understand how it had happened. I felt my arms and legs might fly off at any moment, and I would find myself hyperventilating. A friend on Bob's staff who had also been a political wife gave me the number of a therapist.

Therapy led to certain discoveries about myself that I had never taken the time to make before. The therapist first recommended that I limit my relationship with Bob and work through some of my own personal problems. The process helped me face that I had become consumed by Bob's needs and career goals, and allowed me to stop taking responsibility for him and start taking responsibility for myself. Bob and I had a tight symbiotic relationship that was hard to crack. If I hadn't found a good therapist, we probably would have been locked in the relationship much longer.

Divorce is difficult under any circumstances, but divorcing a congressman was another level of difficult. I took my divorce file to two different lawyers, both of whom held onto it and never filed. After they had each sat on it for several months, I eventually retrieved my file, angry. I could understand how Houston's old-boy network might have prevented them from filing, but a part of me knew my rights were being abused. I felt I was being jerked around by lawyers more concerned about Bob's reelection than my need for a divorce. Thankfully, a female lawyer filed for me, and I was granted a divorce in June of 1977. A couple of months later, Bob married Celia Morris.

AN EXPERIMENTAL WALK DOWN MEMORY LANE

In 1976, at Shelby's suggestion, Bill and I got together to write a joint memoir about the "different trips" we had taken during the previous decades. Bill had been productive when we were married; Bob had been productive when we were married as well. One day Shelby made this point, suggesting that Bill and I write a joint memoir together. I was free to do a project, and Sarah and I had been visiting Austin regularly to see Sidney, Shelby, and Willie. Most of the time Bill would join us for a meal, so we were on good terms. He agreed that the project sounded interesting.

Bill had been an active member of the counterculture during the sixties, experimenting with drugs and alternative lifestyles, while I had done the congressional wife thing. We thought the contrast would be illuminating. Ann Buchwald, Art Buchwald's wife, was a literary agent, so I called her for advice about how to proceed. Ann and I both knew that Bill had a reputation for nonperformance (he hadn't been able to publish anything of note since *The Gay Place*); she told me to work with him for a few days to see how it went before thinking about a contract.

Bill and I agreed to write the book at my house in Houston,

since it was big and private enough for our needs. At forty-six, he was a wreck. He had been doing speed and other drugs for so many years that he had false teeth, he was nearly bald and blind, and he complained of impotence. I thought a strict schedule would be best: I would provide the groceries, and we would work from nine to noon, with a break for lunch; then we would work for several hours in the afternoon. It was a good idea, but it completely didn't work. In the mornings, Bill simply refused to get up, never emerging from his room. He had brought an assistant, Judy Dale, with him; she and I would wait for him to appear each morning. When he didn't show, we'd find him still asleep in his room. I tried to write, using my journals to fashion a time line for each year.

After several days of this, I asked Bill what was going on. He said he needed speed to write. Impatient to get on with it, I called every person I knew who might have been able to get some crystal meth. Each person I spoke to said that their contacts had either quit using or were already dead. I asked Bill if he could substitute cocaine for meth, and he said cocaine wouldn't cut it. The writing experiment was not going well.

One day Bill noticed that I had quit smoking. I explained that I had quit through hypnosis, and he wanted to try it too. We made an appointment. The hypnotist asked Bill if there was anything specific he wanted to work on, and Bill told him that he wanted to quit smoking and become more productive.

I interjected, "How about your kleptomania?"

Bill said, "No, I want to keep that."

As soon as the hypnotist began to speak, I went under and got my stop-smoking message reinforced. But as we got into the elevator to leave, Bill pulled out a cigarette and lit it. When I protested, Bill simply said, "It didn't work." He didn't really want to quit tobacco, crystal meth, or any other self-defeating habits.

Soon Bill and Judy made a trip to Austin so Bill could make his required report to his probation officer. While they were gone, I cleaned house. I found one sheet of paper on which Bill had started a time line. I also discovered that he had taken the pistol my father had given me. It looked like a German Luger, but it was really a pellet gun—it was intimidating enough to ward off an intruder, which is why I kept it around. He had also taken a couple other inconsequential items. The idea that Bill had been prowling through my stuff made me extremely angry, and having experienced his snooping in the past, I wasn't about to let this one slide. When he returned I confronted him. Insulted and angry, he left the house during the night. That was the last time I saw him alive.

ENDINGS BRING BEGINNINGS

Billy Lee Brammer died on February 11, 1978, of a methamphetamine overdose. Sidney got the call. By then she was living in Austin and had been spending a lot of time with Bill, worrying about him constantly. The day before, on February 10, my brother Leslie had died as well, when a blood clot hit his heart. I received the news of Bill's death immediately after my brother's funeral and got straight on a plane. Sidney, Shelby, Willie, and Bill's sister, Rosa LeMae Gunnell, had already handled the funeral arrangements in Austin.

Even though nobody was too surprised that Bill had overdosed, his death still came as a shock. It was horribly sad to watch my children bury their forty-eight-year-old father. The funeral attracted people from all walks of life, from all over Austin—a testament to Bill's life and appeal. The wake was held at the Raw Deal, Bill's favorite eatery, where he ran a tab. Afterward we gathered at Sidney's apartment and told Billy Lee stories, laughing a lot, a tribute to his sense of humor and a healing mechanism for us. Bill was memorialized in the *Washington Post* on June 18, 1978, by his friend Ronnie Dugger:

> Bill Brammer, the author of *The Gay Place,* one of the few great American political novels and the only one that has Lyndon Johnson as its hero, died at 48 last February of acute methamphetamine intoxication, an accidental overdose. Evidently he had been lying in bed reading a book, his shoes off. About 5 o'clock

> in the morning a friend, knocking at his door but getting no answer, went on in, found him gasping, and gave him mouth-to-mouth resuscitation, but could not save him.
>
> Many hundreds came to his funeral, for he was much loved, and he had come to mean something about the contemporary period no one has yet fully understood.

In the next two months, both Daddy Noah and my mother died. I was crushed. My entire immediate family and first husband were now gone. But during all the stress and sadness I never shut down, because my children supported me entirely. We spent a lot of time together in Austin and Houston. The group therapy I was involved in helped immeasurably as well. I took comfort in the fact that I was working and had enough money. These things were what got me through that emotional and difficult time.

The death of my parents brought the end of ties to McAllen, "City of Palms." Bill's death brought the dread, which had been a constant in the lives of all his loved ones, to an end, and marked the beginning of a progression of achievements for each of our children.

BECOMING MYSELF

In 1977, I emerged from divorce as a forty-six-year-old fifties girl who had been altered by the sixties, the Vietnam War, the women's movement, Buddhism, yoga, and three years of psychotherapy. And I had my real estate license. I was empowered and humbled at the same time. I was smarter, softer, and more confident.

Sarah and I were stuck in the boonies of Harris County, twenty-five miles north of Houston, where Sarah was still in middle school. Fortunately, I had a job working as a "transportation consultant" (lobbyist) for George Mitchell, owner of The Woodlands, an environmentally correct development in Montgomery County, until Sarah started attending the High School for the Performing and Visual Arts in Houston. My job was to organize a small town near The Woodlands to form a delegation to go to Austin to lobby the state of Texas for a widened and extended highway. During this time, I fixed up a little shack I had received in the property settlement, rented out the big house for income, and bought a little two-bedroom condo in the Montrose area near Sarah's school. Sarah and I had a "country" place and a "city" place.

Houston was awash with oil money in the seventies. Saudi sheiks were a common sight in downtown Houston, walking around in their white caftans, carrying their briefcases. These were the days of

Urban Cowboy and all the guys were trying to look like John Travolta in the movie. Real estate was inflated. Disco music throbbed from the clubs. Cocaine, alcohol, and pot were the drugs of choice. The freeways were clogged and dangerous, and "road rage" shootings were not uncommon. Sarah and I were in the central city where we had a comfortable, fun existence during her high school years. The condominium had a swimming pool and we knew all the young gay men who were our neighbors. Many of them were Mexican nationals who moved to Houston because their parents couldn't accept their homosexuality, which was painful for them and their parents. One of them, a bright, good-looking young man named Greg Guefen, had sold the condo to me and we became good friends. He asked me to help him with his business since we were both agents. I worked for him a short time before he killed himself over a love affair.

His parents and clients came to Houston with many questions and I was the only one who could help them. They were all wonderful people who owned property in Houston which I managed for them. The young man's parents owned a big shopping center on the southwest freeway along with some other properties. They were a wonderful family, and we spent a lot of time together over the next two years traveling back and forth between the United States and Mexico. The family helped me with my rusty Spanish and I helped them with their English. It was a good relationship. But after Sarah left in 1982 for New York University, I yearned to be back in Austin, where Willie and Sidney were living.

Willie and I had always enjoyed cooking together, and we often talked about opening a modest restaurant with good food and an Austin feel. I sold the shack to the same person who had bought the big house, and I moved to Austin with a little wad of money to manifest our vision. We leased an old wooden building in East Austin near our produce and meat sources because we wanted fresh, unprocessed food. Nadine's was born. We had the best jukebox in town. It was an exhausting amount of work but I had fun with all the wonderful people who came there. Musicians Marcia Ball,

Butch Hancock, and Jerry Jeff and Susan Walker came often. Local politicians, many state employees, and artists were regulars, along with people who had known me in Houston. Malou Flato, known for her marvelous tile murals, for whom we named the "Malou Salad," came for her special salad every day. Photographer extraordinaire Ave Bonar became my great friend, and she has continued to take photos of me through the years. She was on the road with Ann Richards campaigning for governor when she photographed Ann and me in Manhattan at the Lone Star Roadhouse.

Nadine's quickly became a hangout for Austin artists. I had an exhibit each month of various artists' work and helped with publicity for them. It was my forum. I would sit with them and listen to complaints about the Austin Arts Commission playing favorites when it came to funding artists. I encouraged them to organize. Having a restaurant is a great political tool. Politics is "hanging out" with people. Add food and you have a winning combination. With the help of many, we organized and gained the attention of the mayor, and we got the city charter changed. I was appointed to the Arts Commission. I served until the first Bush recession hit and the restaurant had to be sold. By then I was broke after paying off everyone except myself. I had been forced to self-finance the sale of my property in Houston because banks don't make loans on flood plain property—especially to a "feme sole." I wasn't worried after the sale of the restaurant because I still held a $35,000 note from my Houston buyer. But he declared bankruptcy as the recession deepened and just like that the note was worthless. Jobs in Austin disappeared as the recession worsened so I called my friends Betty Dooley and Ann Brinkley, who were in D.C. and ready to help me find a job. Before I left Austin and headed back to D.C., Robert Benton, the filmmaker of renown (*Bonnie and Clyde*, *Kramer vs. Kramer*, *Superman*), called to tell me he was coming to Austin to make a film called *Nadine*. Robert is a consummate artist, and he had been a close friend of mine and Bill's when we were young and living in Austin. He had used Shelby in two of his films: *Kramer vs. Kramer* and *Places in the Heart*, when she was living in New

York, and now *Nadine* in Austin. When Sidney was born, Robert had come with Bill Brammer to the hospital to take us home. After he finished filming *Nadine*, he encouraged Sidney to move to New York to pursue work in film. She took his advice, and he took the time to introduce her to people in the business in NYC. The premiere of *Nadine* was in Austin. Robert thanked me for the use of my name, and I couldn't have had a more entertaining dinner partner at the premiere than one of the stars of the film, Rip Torn. No matter how tough and precarious life has been at times, I always had good things happening around me.

The fun stopped and looking for work in D.C. began in 1987. It was a dark time financially and a good time to reconnect with friends in D.C. Having good female friends in D.C. made the search for a job bearable. I lived alternately with Betty Dooley, who founded the Women's Research and Education Institute in D.C., and Ann Brinkley, my former neighbor who still had an antique store in Georgetown. I signed up with a temp agency and realized I was a 56-year-old dinosaur —an anachronism when it came to finding a job. But after looking for a couple of months, I found one working for the Older Women's League. As assistant to the director, my consciousness was raised about the plight of older women. It was a dreary job, however, and fate intervened again, springing me from the job in the latter part of 1987.

Shelby's boyfriend at the time opened a restaurant in NYC's West Village which he named Nadine's, and Sarah and Shelby were involved in it. Nadine's wanted me to be the "real Nadine" at Nadine's. It was an opportunity to mix with people and have fun again and be with my daughters in NYC. I happily moved to NYC in November of 1987. The restaurant, at 99 Bank Street, was open and good-feeling. Red velvet drapes on tall open windows, mock-elegant furnishings, nice-sized bar, all on one level. Sarah was the hostess and "Nadine's" became her stage. Sarah said it "looked like Mrs. Haversham's dining room if it had been a bordello." A large tile portrait of one of my Duchess of Palms photos hung above the bar. My spirits rose —I had an apartment and a job where I could enjoy myself and my three daughters in the same city. My fortune cookie on May 13, 1988, said "You are headed in the right direction."

The sense of humor and slightly naughty ambiance accompanied by unpretentious food made Nadine's popular. Texans who knew me and my family wanted to meet at Nadine's. I did publicity for the restaurant and let my friends from Texas and D.C. know about my new location. Many Austin artists and friends from D.C. and Texas showed up frequently to meet me for dinner at the restaurant. I was incredibly lucky to have an apartment in the East Village that was owned by friends who didn't live in NYC anymore but were hanging onto it. It was a large apartment with lots of exposed brick, three bedrooms, and full kitchen for $350 per month—a miracle! I could walk across town in twenty minutes and be at Shelby's apartment in the West Village near Nadine's. My apartment building even had a small elevator that worked most of the time. Since Austin was so depressed economically at the time, artists were moving to New York to pursue whatever they could find. Doris Hargrave, an actress from *The Whole Shootin' Match* and friend of mine and my daughters, left Austin and became my apartment-mate. We had the perfect setup: a bedroom for each of us and a guest room for company. Our little guest room accommodated our visiting children and friends who couldn't afford hotels. Although the apartment didn't evoke memories of William Powell's and Myrna Loy's exquisite apartment in *The Thin Man*, it was perfect for making people comfortable and conducive to good times. Bob Eckhardt, divorced and recuperated from his stroke in 1985, and I had become friends again while I was in D.C. He came to New York often to see Sarah and eat in a convivial atmosphere. I didn't have the money to blow on friends, but I had a place for them to stay, so they often took me to see and do things I wouldn't ordinarily have done. I always took them on the Circle Line tour excursion around Manhattan Island, and I never tired of taking the cruise. I was treated to a night at the Blue Note to hear Stephane Grappelli and saw Cirque du Soleil, and went to the Carlyle to hear Bobby Short and saw the Christmas show and the Rockettes at Radio City Music Hall.

In August of 1988, I contracted Salmonella from eating eggs Benedict and found that it is serious business for older people. I was fifty-seven and had a hard time getting rid of it. I needed a job with benefits. I walked by New York University every day and I applied for a job. I had no degree, which was a handicap; however, NYU was interested in hiring me. But there would be a lapse of about two months before I could go on the payroll. Being without a job in NYC was a scary situation, but ultimately a learning experience. In order to keep my stress level down, Shelby and I walked around Washington Square Park every day. I exercised with Jane Fonda's *Prime Time Workout* video if it was raining. Daily doses of Ram Dass tapes and M. Scott Peck reminded me to set aside my ego and expectations and stay in the present. I did some temp work that provided a chance to know women from many ethnicities. Journal entry, June 5, 1989, NYC—

> Made my way by bus to my job. It's always a surprise when you 'temp.' Vantage Press turned out to be a dingy building housing large rooms lined with filing cabinets and enormous rolodexes. After typing numerous letters I realized it is one of those 'publishing houses' that charges people for printing and binding their book. What a scam! I worked with black women from everywhere. My only advantage there is that I type fast, so I'm paid twice what they are making and that's not much. All these workers have one another. They've devised ways to amuse themselves and have fun regardless of the 'brain dead' job and shitty attitude of our immediate superior, a young white speedy woman. Ah well, this too will pass. Not too soon.

Ann Richards and I had known each other since we were young wives in our twenties. She was a beautiful natural blond. She and David had been having children and politicking at the grassroots level in Dallas during the years I was a congressional wife. In November of 1988, Shelby and I were waiting for a bus on Second Avenue when I spotted four women in full-length fur coats standing across the street, a very unusual sight on Second Avenue. One of the women was Ann and she was running in the primary for governor of Texas. Both of us were surprised to see each other and I told her another friend of hers named Mary Rich Adams and I had been planning a fund-raiser at Nadine's for her. Approximately a year later on October 30, 1989, with the help of Mary Adams, we had a fund-raiser at Nadine's. We raised $1,000 after expenses for Ann. Her candidacy activated many young Texans in New York. Katherine DeFoyd, a close family friend, was working for Mayor David Dinkins when we started planning a bigger fund-raiser for Ann. She recruited other professional women who helped immeasurably in the planning stage. The Lone Star Roadhouse in midtown Manhattan was reserved and it was scheduled for September 18, 1990.

Ann was on a tight schedule the night of the event and we were notified she would be late. We had sent out hundreds of invitations to be sure we'd have a crowd to pay for the event and give the rest to her campaign. Thanks to showbiz know-how, a script for a mock debate was written by Shelby for Ann (played by Sarah Eckhardt) and "Claytie" Williams (Ken Hardeman). Shelby and I found the perfect white wig for Sarah to wear. By the time Ann showed, there were 175–200 "Texpatriots," New Yorkers, and young volunteers waiting to welcome her. We knew how to give a good party. And Ann was impressed. She made a good speech and then auctioned off stuff, like a gavel from the Texas House. Afterwards, Ann said to me, "How did you do this?" We were able to give her $10,000 after expenses.

Some time during this uncertain period, Robert Benton and I had lunch. Journal entry, April 28, 1989, NYC—

> Met Robert at his office and went by to see Sidney on the floor below his office. Walked to Russian Tea Room and had chefs' salad (cut up in small pieces like Robert likes it) and a white wine spritzer. Robert looks slim and cute in his checkered coat. He wanted to talk about the 50's and we talked about how we never confronted our wives, husbands, lovers. We were innocent

> and manipulative and naïve with a sophistication at the same time. He concentrated on how did I feel giving up my art, my schooling, etc., for my husband? He's working on something and says I help him more than I realize. He said my life is my art. At least I'm a compulsive journal keeper.

New York University offered me a job and I took it. It was in the services office, where students came to be counseled by academic advisors regarding their degree plans, and if they were having any personal problems they could walk down the hall for help. Phillip Moore, the psychologist I got to know, had me take the Strong-Campbell Interest Inventory to ascertain what kind of work I should be doing. Journal entry Nov. 1, 1989, NYC—

> Phillip Moore got my Strong-Campbell test back and called me in to explain it to me. He asked me 'What have you done besides be a secretary?' After I told him, he said 'work up a resume and get a head hunter.' He asked me about my role in my husband's political life. I gave a quick history. Basically, he said I am an 'introvert intuitive type' and should be working for a broadcaster or public speaker or something like political work.

The test simply validated all the things I had been doing my whole life. But at that time, I was working as secretary to the Dean of the College of Arts and Sciences at New York University and watching the Texas governor's race.

My daughters and I knew we needed a house in Austin as a base. Our furniture, etc., was in storage. We knew it was a good time to buy a house because Austin was flat economically. My good friend, Pat Burnett, a broker, had submitted several contracts for us in the process of finding an owner-financed one. She called one day and sent photos, and we pooled our money to come up with a $5,000 down payment. We closed on the deal in New York in November of 1990, and drove to Texas during the Christmas holidays to see it and move our stuff into it. During our brief stay, I was offered a job by Jo Campbell, a Public Utility Commissioner whom I had met in Washington. Although I felt I would probably have a job with the Richards administration, I accepted Jo's offer.

In 1991, the economy was still flat in Austin. Property taxes were low, traffic was light, there was less pollution, Barton Springs still clean, and friends still had time to visit. I looked forward to my job with the state agency, which had been created in the seventies to protect consumers from being gouged by the electric utilities and the telephone companies. Three commissioners, appointed by the sitting governor, rule on issues that are complicated and technical. It is quasi-judicial, with the companies' lawyers and the agency's lawyers presenting their respective cases to the commissioners, who vote to determine the case. The governor, who has received contributions from the companies regulated by the agency, appoints the commissioners. Not surprisingly, the commissioners often rule according to which side the sitting governor favors. I retired from the state as soon as I hit sixty-five and immediately went to work part-time for Molly Ivins, the columnist whom I had known for many years. Finally, I had the job which was my dish—as prescribed by the results of the Strong-Campbell test I had taken at New York University. I worked in the newsroom of the *Fort Worth Star-Telegram*, publisher of Molly's column, which was syndicated in many national newspapers. It was wonderful relating to Molly. She was the most brilliant, fun-loving, kind, extraordinary human being I have ever experienced. I am fortunate to have worked for her for five and a half years before retiring at age seventy. Molly's and Ann's and Lady Bird's deaths have been huge losses for me over the past two years.

THE NINETIES AND THE CIRCLE CLOSES

When the whole family migrated to Austin in the nineties, Bob Eckhardt was divorced from Celia Morris and living by himself in a big old yellow house with a giant old oak tree in the backyard, where he had an outside fire pit to cook on and a tree house where he could sit and sip his Scotch. He resumed his family's habit of going to Barton Springs when the temperature was eighty-five degrees or higher. After a swim, he drove recklessly home in his banged-up pickup to have that afternoon Scotch. His house was crammed with books, old furniture, drawings, paintings, and photographs. He always seemed to live in the eighteenth century; he had a woodstove installed in his living room for heat. He learned to use a computer, sort of. With his big, sausage-like fingers, he pecked out a book on the War Powers Act called *Who Decides War*. He was working on it when he died.

Bob's backyard was a welcoming, haphazard assortment of tables made from old sewing machines and marble slabs. He loved to have company, especially someone who would have a drink with him. After my daughters and I moved back to Austin, we had many family gatherings in that backyard. I had returned for a job opportunity, Shelby had returned to school, Sarah had come to go to law school, and Sidney had come to establish a home base while working in the film business in NYC. Willie had stayed in Austin during our sojourns in NYC. Orissa and Rosalind and their children made yearly treks from New Orleans and Colorado to see their father. A closeness among us grew to the benefit of all of us.

Bob loved having Sarah in town, and when she graduated from UT Law School and the LBJ School of Public Affairs simultaneously while working part-time for the county, he was so happy. They spent many hours talking about the law together. He always had plenty of women around who would drive him to parties and endure his presumption that they were there to serve him. It was interesting for me to talk to Bob as an adult friend without anger. He liked to talk politics with me, and he liked having my attention. We still shared many friends and family, and a sense of humor, which made for good times. The war in Bosnia became an obsession for him and it led to his book *Who Decides War*.

Sarah married Kurt M. Sauer and Bob lived to see his grandson, Henry Eckhardt Sauer, born in January of 2001. Bob died of a massive stroke on November 13, 2001.

Not long before he died, he looked me hard in the eye and said, "Sarah got the best of you and the best of me and she would make a good legislator." She won her first political race for Travis County Commissioner in Precinct Two, in 2006, in the same district in which Ann Richards had won her first political race.

Afterword

Bob didn't live to see the Iraq War, but he was prescient about the future of the country and possible efforts to subvert the Constitution. He was an eighteenth-century man and a constitutional lawyer who could foresee the pitfalls we are now facing. That's why he was writing a book about *Who Decides War.* He lived long enough to see the attack on the World Trade Center on September 11, 2001, but didn't live to see how we got into this war. He would've been outraged at how it was contrived and how the government has set the stage for further conflict in the future.

In early 2002, President George H. W. Bush called me to get the names and addresses of Bob's daughters so he could write letters to them. During that conversation, we caught up with each other's doings. He was gracious and charming as always. All three daughters received beautifully written letters from the former president, which they will always treasure.

Unfortunately, Texans had experience with his oldest son, George W. Bush. From that experience, perceptive Texans knew he didn't have the capabilities or intellect for the position of governor, much less president. He has a thin veneer of the grace and charm of his father, but anger underneath it. At the time I talked with his father, his son hadn't had time to make war on Iraq. In 2003, President George W. Bush was touting the "facts" about going to war in Iraq: Saddam Hussein and 9/11, WMDs and nuclear capabilities. Clearly, the son needed some sobering advice from his father who had "been there, done that" in the 1990s with the Persian Gulf War. I felt so strongly that I wrote his father a letter on February 28, 2003, urging him to offer *his* wisdom to his son.

I received a reassuring letter written March 10, 2003, telling me he was "happy to remain on the sidelines" not giving advice to his son and that he had "full confidence in him" and to "have faith." Eighteen days later, on March 28, 2003, the world watched the three-hundred-mile convoy of heavy artillery experiencing sandstorms on their way to Baghdad. And here we are in 2008—thousands of American soldiers killed and injured, hundreds of thousands of civilians killed, the U.S. economy suffering, and we don't know why. Did President Bush and Vice President Cheney and the "neocons" want the oil, or to obtain "positioning" in the Middle East, or to have an endless war maintaining the military-industrial complex in perpetuity? All they had to do was read *World Transformed* by his father and Brent Scowcroft to find out what would happen if they pursued a war in Iraq. They were clear about how difficult it would be:

1) The human losses would be staggering.
2) An exit strategy and stability would be almost impossible due to the tribalism.
3) We would have to rule Iraq—the "Pottery Barn" rule voiced by Colin Powell in his argument against the war dictates that "if you break it, you bought it."

All of the above advice was ignored and all the above predictions have manifested. Why he chose to go along with the darker elements of Cheney and the "neocons" is conjecture that is waiting for the truth that will surely come.

If anyone had the chance to make the world better, it was George W. Bush, especially after 9/11 when the world was on our side. Unfortunately, he chose to be a dishonest, manipulative, hypocritical president, full of hubris. I knew the Bushes as thoughtful, personable people. Bob and I spent good times with them. I am sorry their son is an anomaly and has been a disaster for the world.

At this time in 2008, it is hard to be optimistic about the future. However, when I think of the grit, stamina, and faith my forebears needed to migrate from the east coast to Texas during the past two centuries, I feel confident our country will survive.

Index

PS indicates image in unpaginated photo section